Her Longest Marathon

Her Longest Marathon

A Runner's
Race to Survive

RANDY A. BIRKEN

BLUE DOLPHIN PUBLISHING

Published by Blue Dolphin Publishing, Inc.
P.O. Box 8, Nevada City, CA 95959
Orders: 1-800-643-0765
Web: www.bluedolphinpublishing.com

ISBN: 978-1-57733-226-8 softcover
ISBN: 978-1-57733-241-1 hardcover

Library of Congress Cataloging-in-Publication Data

Birken, Randy A., 1950-
    Her longest marathon : a runner's race to survive / Randy A.
Birken.
        p. cm.
    Includes bibliographical references.
    ISBN 978-1-57733-226-8 (pbk. : alk. paper)
    1. Lance, Joyce—Health. 2. Crash injuries—Patients—United
States—Biography. 3. Long-distance runners—United States—
Biography. I. Title.

RD96.6.L36B57 2008
617.1'028092--dc22
[B]

                                                    2008049711

First printing: December 2008

Cover photo: Courtesy of Joyce Lance
Photo captions in text written by Joyce Lance

Printed in the United States of America

10   9   8   7   6   5   4   3   2   1

Contents

A Note about Joyce Lance

FROM THE TIME OF JOYCE'S INITIAL OFFICE VISIT in 1992, I was impressed with her combination of an easygoing disposition and a fierce dedication to her favorite past-time, long-distance running. Over the following years, she maintained her excellent conditioning and experienced only minor medical issues.

However, in October 2000 Joyce's life took an abrupt turn when she was struck by an automobile and suffered multiple serious injuries, some life-threatening, some disfiguring, and some crippling. The fact that she survived is a testament to her strength and perseverance.

Over the next several years, I saw Joyce for her regular check-ups during which her progress was slow but definite. Although Joyce will never run another marathon, her recovery from the ICU to barely walking to being fully mobile was remarkable. During a recent visit, I suggested that a written account of her experiences would be inspirational. She replied that she would like to tell her story but did not know where to start. I recommended Dr. Randy Birken, a longtime friend and colleague, whose talent and dedication has allowed Joyce to see her wish fulfilled.

Gary Urano, M.D.
Austin, Texas

Introduction

AS UNLIKELY AS IT MAY SEEM, Dr. Gary Urano asked me if I would be interested in writing a book about one of his patients while we were performing surgery, a most unusual setting. While light conversation during an operation helps mitigate the tension for most surgeons, Gary and I would always work together seamlessly, each knowing what instrument to hold or grasp, what knife or scissors to cut with, and what suture to place and tie. As gynecologic surgeons, we were more than compatible as colleagues and friends, but as an operating team where discussions and joke telling were commonplace. Yet, when Gary related the intriguing facts about Joyce, a marathon runner hit by a speeding car, near death, and somehow surviving to function at an almost pre-injury level, my interest was replaced by doubt; I was a fiction writer, not a journalist. But I was a runner and fitness enthusiast and felt a connection with Joyce. However, did I have it within me to investigate the particulars of her story and use a different kind of creativity—writing facts that would appeal to a reader? Little did I know that after meeting Joyce, researching her accident, studying her hospitalizations, reviewing her surgeries, and interviewing many family, friends, co-workers, and medical personnel, that I, the writer, would be enlightened and edified by her equanimity and irreproachable belief in personal survival; but it was her forgiveness that was most inspiring, an ability to transcend what had happened to her and move on while still counting her blessings. That attitude, that personal philosophy, that individual strength, along with a genuine desire to help others, will remain most memorable and heartening. Perhaps, Mohandas Gandhi said it most eloquently with his simple words: "The weak can never forgive. Forgiveness is the attribute of the strong."

While driving to the hospital for an early morning surgery, I listened to a local radio station airing for the series "This I Believe" and knew that I must contribute what I had learned not only from Joyce, but from many other patients. Luckily, my essay was accepted by KUHF in Houston and recorded at a later date:

> I believe in the power of personal survival.
>
> As a practicing physician for the past twenty-seven years, I have witnessed patients' extraordinary emotional resiliency to live in spite of tragic events. A typical day in a gynecologist's office includes the usual array of complaints; menstrual disorders, tiredness, aches and pains, and of course, the ubiquitous problem of weight gain; but occasionally there are those patients who demonstrate a courageous ability to move on with their lives even after severe physical or mental trauma. I witness a true desire to live, not based on acquiescence or denial, but a decision to live their lives as fully as possible while carrying the heavy emotional burdens of personal tragedy.
>
> Such times do more than just impress me ... they reinforce my belief in human survival. These patients do not seek sympathy or pity, just an acceptance of life's vicissitudes and uncertainties.
>
> An example of such a patient includes the marathon runner hit by a drunken driver. While suffering disabling fractures and internal injuries requiring years of painful rehabilitation, she is able to forgive the offender and be thankful to walk and be productive; the rape patient who is able to transcend a heinous personal violation to help others who have suffered similar horrors; the cancer survivor who cherishes every day with renewed appreciation and an attitude uncompromisingly positive; and the mother who has lost a son to war, yet keeps his spirit alive by living her life completely without anger or self-pity.
>
> Louisa May Alcott, author of *Little Women,* once said: "I am not afraid of storms for I am learning how to sail my ship."
>
> My patients, who choose to survive after misfortune and catastrophe, more than inspire; their acts of courage validate the human spirit, an inner sense deep within all of us, and an appreciation of the great gift of life itself.
>
> This I believe.

Rollo May, the great twentieth-century American existential psychologist, wrote, "Life comes from physical survival; but the good life comes from what we care about." While too simplistic for the complexity of one person, his words aptly capture the quintessence and spirit of Joyce Lance, the core of her resilience and the humanism of her being.

Randy and I originally met at a coffee shop in Spring, Texas.
Our common purpose was formed and Randy began writing the book.
Hurricane Ike damaged our coffee shop so we found a new place
for this picture. Randy has definitely put
my thoughts and our message in the book.

Chapter One

Memorial Park

IT WAS UNUSUAL for Joyce to do a long run on Friday morning. Sunday was when she ran fifteen to twenty-five miles—one long run per week, enough training for the next marathon—but today was different—four-thirty A.M.—and the air was unseasonably warm, thick, and humid for a Houston October morning. Joyce never wore long running pants even on chilly days, only shorts, maybe a jacket or gloves if it was extremely cold.

The best place to park her Nissan Maxima was at the well-lit tennis center; usually, the same vehicles were there. While Joyce didn't know the names of the other nocturnal runners, they all recognized one another—a silent nod or a slightly raised hand was their greeting as they passed on the running track—members of a select group of people, dedicated to their predawn runs. Did they ever wonder about their ages or careers, or why they would run at four-thirty every morning? A natural curiosity, but did it matter? They were all runners, drawn passionately to a sport pitting the physical against the mental—the competition within—a strange obsession to push physiologic limits as inner thoughts beat in cadence with a pumping heart—a trance induced by brain neurochemicals and endorphins soothing primal emotions as well as painful memories. Maybe it was the high they sought and shared, an affair of the spirit bordering on the metaphysical. Perhaps, it was their discipline, a committed drive defining their lives.

Joyce locked her car and put the key in a magnetized plastic container, placing it safely under the car. No phone or ID—just her body and mind as well as the appropriate accoutrements—shirt, shorts, and running shoes. This was her time; and while an un-selfish person, she shared it with no one but herself—a time to move through the morning air uninterrupted, free from family or work—a meditative zone while communing with nature. Pre-running stretching, followed by a cleansing deep breath before starting the ritual—one foot stepping forward and the other fol-lowing, slowly at first, then quicker with longer strides as the heart beat faster and the lungs expanded deeper in unison—a human machine with all its parts becoming one—efficient, fluid, natu-ral—a moving body with balance, awareness, and energy against the dark air above and the soft crushed granite path below.

A beautiful track, meandering through White Oak, Bald Cy-press, Sycamore, Yaupon Holly, Willow Oak, and Loblolly Pine, named for a well-known Houston civic leader, the Seymour Lieberman Running Trail was part of Memorial Park, a large piece of land offering picnic tables, softball fields, tennis courts, swim-ming pool, golf course, hiking, off-road cycling, soccer, rugby, and horse back riding—an outdoor oasis located conveniently between downtown and uptown Houston. On her long runs, Joyce veered off the track, past the Arboretum and Nature Center, under the train tracks, and towards the 610 West Loop, then south to San Felipe, east through River Oaks, and back to the park—her long run completed. Only this was Friday morning, not Sunday. She never missed a long run on the weekend, but unexpected business in Dallas on Saturday and Sunday necessitated a change of plans. Twice around the running path was six miles, her usual weekday run, but this early morning was different, yet it felt the same. The foliage was hidden by early morning shadows, but Joyce knew what grew in this subtropical forest—Winged Elm, Virginia Creeper, Rusty Blackhaw, and Red Mulberry.

Her thoughts were private, like her life, but she was drawn to be outdoors, something familiar from her upbringing in rural Minnesota. Her mind flashed to the past. There were twenty-seven students in her one room schoolhouse guarded by two outhouses. Joyce learned quickly, and by the time sixth grade came around, she knew the lessons by heart; but it was her parents, Danish and German descendants, who stressed education to their five children. Farm chores needed to be done, but homework came first. Tenaciously embracing her parents' work ethics, Joyce never relaxed until all responsibilities were met. Reality returned. Even now, leisure came after everything was completed. Maybe, her running was fundamental to the same concept.

When married, she ran with her husband during his military stint. They were high school sweethearts and wed at eighteen. When he was drafted into the Army and sent to Germany, Joyce continued to run. When they returned to the States, she finished college; but they moved often—South Dakota, West Virginia, Florida, and Honduras. She never stopped outdoor exercise, even when a bodyguard, armed with a machete and on horseback, accompanied her during runs in Central America. After ten years of marriage, Peter was born; but six years later, she was divorced, and only her running remained, a passion as well as therapy, while she raised a son and made it on her own. She learned to be resilient, especially after her youngest sister died from Hodgkin's disease. No one could take the running away from her existence, not until this Friday morning when she planned to do her long run instead of her accustomed Sunday; but her obstinate belief in surviving, a tenet that helped her through the worst of times, providing physical and mental strength, would come into play once again, this time during a tougher, more challenging set of events, something she never experienced before—something more difficult than an up-hill marathon with powerful headwinds and blinding rain. She didn't know it yet, but she was about to begin her longest marathon.

The traffic on the West Loop was constant, even near five o'clock this morning. Joyce turned south on the feeder road running along the inside lane. What were her thoughts at this time? Her business in Dallas; the ten-thirty meeting at the bank; visiting with her best friend, Lila; seeing her two-month-old granddaughter, Ally; or greeting her best friend from Minnesota, Connie, who was arriving in Houston on Sunday? Or nothing at all, just her mind and body in a primal rhythm, running for the joy of being alive and the thrill of the future?

The Jaguar exited the Loop, a late evening with friends coming to an end, neither machine nor human seeing each other. How did it happen? Why, after so many years of running the same route, did the two meet, vehicle versus pedestrian, hard metal and rubber tires hitting soft tissue, strong bones, and well oxygenated blood—an unfair collision between two distinctly opposite precision systems, one alive and complex, the other a machined set of wires, gears, and pistons? Fate, bad luck, or divine intervention? Questions unanswerable to those who knew her—yet Joyce's body lay in a blood bath after being struck at fifty miles an hour, tossed into the air, flying off the windshield and landing one hundred and twenty feet ahead on the hard pavement.

Only Joyce knew—her legs moving instinctively, still trying to run the race of life within her twisted broken body and darkened unconscious mind.

These are some of the medals from the twenty-three marathons that I have run. My grandchildren have adopted some other of my medals.

CHAPTER TWO

EMS—
Matthew, My Hero

IT WAS ALMOST FIVE A.M. and Matthew Sultemeier was waiting for his twenty-four hour shift to end. A slow night, some calls for transports to a hospital, one auto accident near the Galleria, nothing serious. Matthew liked his job, a well-trained EMS specialist, but some people took advantage of the Houston Fire Department, demanding an ambulance for minor problems. It was the serious accidents that required his expertise—and he was good at it.

The 911 operator took the call and triaged the frantic motorist to the central dispatch located downtown. A fireman, recovering from an injury three months before, put the information into his computer. The captain on duty checked the status of the two closest firehouses. One ambulance was out on a run, but Matthew's unit was available. He called both firehouses knowing that at least one non-medical unit would arrive at the accident scene with Matthew's medical unit close behind.

"Auto-pedestrian accident, feeder road 610 northbound, Woodway exit."

Matthew put his can of soda down and headed for the ambulance with his sleepy partner in tow. Only five minutes away, Matthew thought; but something didn't quite click—auto-pedestrian accident on the feeder?—maybe on Westheimer, near the Galleria, or on Richmond, a boulevard of bars, clubs, and dance halls, night action that never stopped. 610 feeder road? Auto-pedestrian? Whatever.

Matthew is my hero!
He was on duty at EMS and
came to the accident site.
For my second birthday after
the accident, many of my Klein
Bank friends "found"
Matthew and surprised me
when he attended the party.
Matthew and I have stayed in
contact ever since. He is truly a
special person in my life
and will remain so.

The unit from the other firehouse was already at the scene. Matthew was quick to assess. Next to a new Jaguar was a woman, gesticulating wildly with her hands. Matthew had seen it all—the minor fender benders to the gruesome wrecks—bodies torn up from glass and metal, heads decapitated. He didn't recall when he learned to detach emotion and maintain professionalism. He used to take it home with him and sleep fitfully, but now it was routine, part of his job.

The humid morning air brushed his cold, air-conditioned skin. When will cooler weather come? It's late October, too hot for this time of year. He turned on his flashlight and saw it—an Asics running shoe, alone and sitting on its side, divorced from the foot that gave it life and motion. Matthew saw the contorted runner's body lying in a wet pool of blood, body fluids, and the street's oily dampness. He strolled towards the lifeless figure and looked up at his fellow fireman talking to the motorist; but instead of a greeting, the fireman raised his hand and pointed his thumb down towards the warm pavement—a universal sign—simple but powerful—a gesture of defeat, a beacon for death. Matthew acknowledged the omen, but it was his job to determine the victim's status—it was his duty; but he realized that a body hit by a moving car at fifty miles per hour, thrown one hundred and twenty feet from the impact, had little chance to be alive, let alone survive, even if a trace of life remained.

Matthew didn't expect to find a woman—why was she running by herself at this hour? Instinctively, he felt for a carotid pulse, assuming the vessel was quiet and still. While her warm skin didn't surprise him, the strong beat of the artery did. He stood up and stared at the deformed body. His eyes widened. Could it be? Her legs, they were moving, but not in a convulsing way, but rhythmic—like they were trying to run. Matthew shook his head. How could they be moving? What kind of person did these legs belong to? He turned and signaled to his partner to bring the stretcher. The two men secured her neck with a cervical collar and placed the body on a backboard. Even if he didn't get her to the hospital alive, at least she'd make a good organ donor.

Expertly, they moved her into the ambulance without further displacing her broken spine and drove towards Hermann Hospital's Trauma Center, one of two Level Three ERs at the Texas Medical Center, the largest medical complex in the world. The heart monitor indicated complications of blood loss and trauma, low blood pressure and a rapid, weak pulse. Matthew placed a tube into her trachea and began assisted breathing. He opened the IV tubing to maximum flow while the ambulance's siren played a disharmonious song to passersby as its pitch changed—a law of physics, the Doppler effect. Adroitly, the ambulance navigated the complex streets of the medical center, passing tall buildings belonging to the forty-two institutions, including thirteen hospitals and eleven schools, on an eight-hundred-acre campus—four thousand physicians and over sixty-five thousand employees worked there—a city within a city with its own transportation system and zip code.

Matthew's partner notified the triage nurse of their estimated time of arrival and the extent of the victim's injuries. They would be ready, Matthew thought—they could handle anything. Matthew opened the rear door while the ambulance backed into the dock. Two nurses and one intern pulled the stretcher and rolled it past the automated doors into the well-lit ER corridor. Matthew stared as the victim disappeared into the chambers of the trauma center. He wondered about this woman, legs still trying to run, after massive trauma.

Matthew slept restlessly that night.

Chapter Three

Accident Report

Texas Peace Officer's Accident Report

Place where accident occurred:
Harris County, Houston
Major auto-Pedestrian

Road on which accident occurred:
1000 West Loop South

Date of accident:
10-20-2000, Friday 4:35 A.M.

Unit No. 1—Motor Vehicle:
1999 Silver Jaguar, XJS

Unit No. 2:
Pedestrian

Light Condition:
Dark-Lighted

Weather:
Clear

Surface Condition:
Dry

Type of Surface:
Concrete

Houston Police Department Motor Vehicle Accident Report

UNIT NO. 1 REMARKS:

I'm not sure what lane I was in. All of a sudden, I see the lady's face and I hit her. She came out of nowhere.

UNIT NO. 2 REMARKS:

No statement

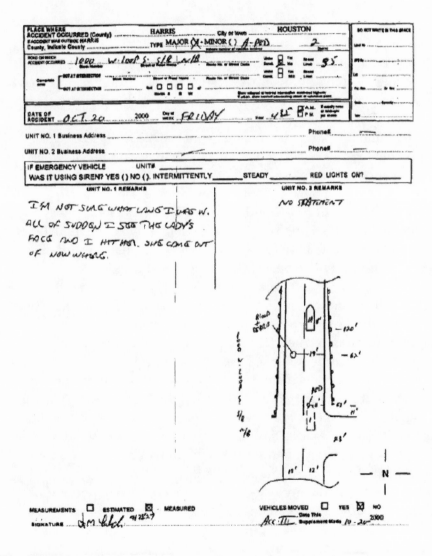

CHAPTER FOUR

Joyce

As I LOOK AROUND ME, I am confused. Where am I? Why am I in a strange bed in a strange place? Why are all of these people that I don't know standing around me? My son, Peter, is with these people. What has happened?

I think back to what I last remember. On October 20th, 2000, I set out to run a twenty-mile run. I'm a marathon runner, twenty-three so far. I have run New York City, San Francisco, Avenue of the Giants, Big Sur, St. George, San Antonio, Houston, New Orleans, Marine Corps, Grandma's, and The Woodlands. It was my intention to train and run the Houston Marathon one more time and hopefully qualify for Boston. That would make twenty-five.

After thirty-five years of running, I had decided to stop the long-distance ones. I wanted to qualify and run Boston for my last marathon, then relax and run ten kilometer/five kilometer runs only. My days of running forty-five to seventy miles per week were coming to an end. I love to work out, but I wanted to run shorter distances and take it easy on my knees.

On this particular day, I started my run at about four-thirty AM. I ran out of Memorial Park. My twenty-mile route is a common trail for long distance runners in Houston. My normal schedule was to run six miles a day, Monday through Friday. Sunday was my "long run day" and I ran a minimum of fifteen miles up to thirty miles every Sunday.

Typically, I did my long-distance runs on Sunday morning, but on this particular weekend, I had other plans for the weekend and

These are some of the running numbers from some of the marathons
that I have run. In total I have run twenty-three,
but some have disappeared over the years.

I decided I wanted to do my long run on Friday morning before I went to work. That is all I remember.

I don't know if I finished my run and I don't know what day or what time it is. I don't know why I am in this bed with these people surrounding me and I don't know where I am. I only know that Peter is with me.

I notice that my head doesn't move and that something is holding my head to the bed. Why can't I lift my right arm? As I look down, my legs look like large objects hidden under the blankets. What has happened to my legs? Why can't I move them?

I swish my tongue around my mouth. I can feel some loose teeth. Others are missing. I wonder what my face looks like.

I'm concentrating hard to understand what has happened to me. Suddenly, my thoughts are shocked by the sound of Peter's voice. My attention is drawn back to the people surrounding me and to what my son is saying.

"Mom, you've been in a serious accident while you were running. You've been at the Hermann Hospital Trauma Center for the past three weeks. You'll be living here at the Beacon South Rehabilitation Center for a while so your body can heal and the physical therapists can work with you."

As I listen to Peter, I hear what he says, but I don't understand. Peter explains that the people in the room are the doctors, nurses and physical therapists that will work with me. I look at the group and say, "Okay, I understand, but I'm only going to stay a week, two at the most, so fix as much as you can in that time frame because then I'm leaving. I need to get back to work." Everyone

Peter and his wife, Meghan, with their three children.
Allyson and Clay are Peter's children from a previous marriage.
Peter and Meghan were married in January 2007, and Addisen is
our little "sweetheart." Many times I have said that if I could
"pick a son off a shelf," I would pick Peter. Now I can say, if I could
"pick my family off a shelf," I would choose Peter, Meghan, Allyson,
Clay and Addisen. A family full of love for eath other and others!

nods in agreement and I'm happy with what I have said. I'm in control again and I intend to get well and back to my life, the quicker the better.

The medical team leaves the room and Peter and I are alone. I asked him more questions.

"Mom, you've got a halo on your head that's screwed into your skull. The halo is connected to a body cast that holds your head, neck and back in a fixed position. You broke your back and neck in three places and the halo and body cast are necessary so that your body heals. You had severe injuries to your head. You have a large skin graft on the right side of your scalp which has to be watched carefully so it doesn't start bleeding."

Peter continues. "Your cheekbones and right eye socket were broken and your hair was shaved while they were putting on the halo and doing the skin graft, but now your hair's growing back."

I asked about my teeth. Peter explains that some of my teeth were damaged or knocked out. He tells me that my legs are badly damaged; that the car hit me going about fifty miles per hour, that my initial contact was my knees when the car hit me.

"While you were in the trauma center, you were bleeding a lot from your right hip as well as your head. The doctors did lots of surgeries at the trauma center and they put a rod into your right leg because the femur bone was so badly damaged. Your right knee was smashed and the surgeons put it back together with metal parts and screws."

I heard Peter clearly, but I still didn't understand why my right leg seemed so heavy. Peter continued.

"Your tibia bone was badly crushed. The surgeon tried to put the bone pieces back by placing rods into your leg. The heavy thing you feel is the fixator. It's a piece of equipment holding all the other rods in your bones together." He asks if I want to see the fixator. I told him, no, not yet. I asked Peter about my left leg.

"Mom, you broke your left leg also. Your left knee was also damaged. The surgeon tried to put your knee back together, but he couldn't just yet. Hopefully, it will heal and not require any more surgery."

I still didn't understand the severity of my situation. I thought about all the people who had broken bones, and while it was inconvenient, they went on with their lives. At this point, I saw no reason to change my plans—I need to get better as soon as possible and back to my home, job, and life as quickly as I could.

"Your left arm is broken," Peter continues, "and that's why you have a cast on it. Your right shoulder was dislocated and it caused nerve damage to your shoulder, arm and hand. Your right wrist and arm were also broken." I asked Peter why I can't move my right arm or hand.

"The physical therapist will work to help you learn how to use your right arm and hand."

I don't recall ever thinking that I might not be able to use my extremities. Just two weeks and I'll be back to normal I thought.

A nurse peeks in the door and asks if she could change the dressing on my stomach incision. I didn't know what she was talking about. What else happened? Has Peter not told me everything?

Peter stares at me and turns toward the nurse. "Give us five minutes."

He sits down and leans closer towards me. "Mom, I didn't get time to tell you about your stomach. While you were in the trauma center, you were bleeding internally. You had so many cuts, scrapes, and wounds that the trauma center doctors cut an incision in your stomach to release all the blood. The incision runs from under your rib cage to your pelvic bone. It's deep and goes through all of your muscles and tissues and has to heal on its own from the inside out. The nurse needs to clean the incision several times a day."

No, I thought. I'm not going to let this setback be more than an inconvenience. Peter stands, touches my face, and leaves the room. That's when I saw the sign on the wall across the room: Welcome to Beacon South Rehabilitation Center. November 13, 2000.

Okay, I thought, maybe I won't be fixed by Thanksgiving, but I'll be home for Christmas for sure. I know I will.

CHAPTER FIVE

First Meeting

PEOPLE MILL AROUND THE TRENDY STARBUCKS, just off the North Freeway in Spring, Texas. Which one of the vehicles is hers? Not the fashionable Mini Cooper—too small. What about the new Explorer? Probably not; but a sudden awareness of the handicapped parking spots ends the guessing—maybe just pre-meeting jitters.

The low fat, sugar-free hazelnut latte is hot and sweet. Scanning the room is like guessing her car. What to expect? A fifty-eight year old who looks young, fit, and healthy—or an older-appearing woman still trapped within a body deformed by metal rods, plates, screws, and surgical scars? No customer fits the mold. Maybe she decided not to come—too difficult to relive a devastating chapter of her life, but in the corner sits a tall, curly blond-haired woman, strong rays of sunlight coming through the window showcasing her like a spotlight on a celebrity. Pamphlets, books, and envelops lay neatly on the small table. She turns and smiles when hearing her name, a kindly face followed by a hearty handshake. Guessing her appearance was wrong; would it be the same for other expectations? With the laptop screen open and Word document accessed, the conversation begins, at first choppy on the keyboard, then with a smoother syncopation as Joyce relates the facts. Something is special about this woman—cordial, confident, and open. Maybe it's her unassuming way that is so impressive. There is much to learn from her.

"Here are some of my marathon photos," she says with her chin proudly raised. "This was my last one before the accident."

Tall and thin, the right physique for long strides and carrying a light cargo. In every marathon photo, her face looks the same—calm with barely a sweat; a runner's joy, something protected deeply within, a natural feeling emanating from an inner spirit when the body and mind are whole, a mixture of equanimity and determination.

Joyce opens a photo album. "Look at this, my one-room school house in Minnesota. See the two outhouses?"

Radiantly green grass surrounds the quaint building, a reflection of rural farming values—a testimony to hard work and neatness, unadulterated by highways, factories, or toxins. This was her ethical and moral foundation, the essence of her background.

"My parents stressed education above all, but we needed to do our chores as well." Her eyes gleam. "I loved school and I loved to learn. That's why I finished my college degree when we returned to the States."

Good values and high goals, but it took more than that to survive the trauma she sustained over five years ago.

My one-room, country school. I attended this school
for grades 1 through 6. Approximately 30 students
went to this school each year that I was there

"I didn't remember anything until three weeks later when I was at Beacon for rehab." She smiles again. "Peter was there, he told me what happened."

Peter, a twenty-one-year-old with a two-month-old daughter, now faced agonizingly tough decisions. After almost forty units of blood, emergency exploratory surgery, and resuscitation from cardiovascular shock and collapse, she remained alive. Peter didn't have to tell the doctors yet about organ donation or funeral homes; but it wasn't over, not with his mother's broken back, smashed right hip and leg, fractured left leg, destroyed left knee, multiple upper arm breaks, and a dislocated shoulder.

"All my friends knew I would survive," she says while nodding her head. "'That's Joyce,' my friends told me later." She laughs girlishly. "'We knew you'd never quit.'"

There is no bravado here. Her words are genuine, but more importantly, it's how she says them.

Suddenly, she bows her head. Tears? No. She raises her face, eyes shining with love.

"It was hard on Peter." She sighs. "You know, we've been more than parent and child; we've been best friends as well. Ever since his father and I divorced, we've been there for each other."

The laptop keys click and record, but my mind races with visualizations—mother and child—a relationship without parallels, a heart beating with tenderness and forgiveness. She leans back in her chair.

"Poor Peter. He had great support from my friends, but sometimes my father put too much pressure on him." She sips her tea and gives a pensive stare. "One time he called my Dad." Her voice is lower. "My father was scared, but he probably shouldn't have told him what he did."

Still no tears, but a quiet look, contemplative and serene. She wets her lips. "My father told him that he has his daughter's life in his hands."

I study her nod—a slow one, deliberate and convincing, a gesture of understanding without anger.

"I think it put too much pressure upon him. I mean, he was only twenty-one years old with an infant daughter." She swallows and stares at her cup before continuing. "He's an amazing individual," she says softly. "I've told him many times that if I could have picked a son off of the shelf, he'd be everything that I could ever love and have." She smiles while the keys on the laptop respond. Maternal love—strong, veritable, unconditional.

My latte is cold. Should I order more? No, I'm too absorbed with Joyce's words to get up and disrupt the flow of her conversation.

Joyce shifts in her chair, a slight tug to one leg as if it wasn't quite listening to her command. "When my friends came to see me at rehab, little did I know that not only was my halo showing, as well as my nifty haircut, but my dangling tooth was quite visible. My concern was not for how I looked, but for the people that are so important to me. I didn't want them to see the bad parts of me. I had no doubt that I'd be back and working with them again soon."

Her emails, prior to this meeting, reflected determination and unselfishness, but now it's confirmed on a higher level, an inner spiritual strength, intuitively felt through the interaction of voice, face, and gestures.

She places her hands on the table as if at a séance. Her refined fingers are long and slender. "And so many people continued to see me every day and call. They brought me all kinds of food. When people came to visit, I was always covered up to my neck, but I couldn't hide my halo; I didn't want people to see my injuries." She places her hands on her lap in a delicate feminine move. "I wanted to hear about what was happening in their lives and at work." She shakes her head slowly. "Even though I was injured, I wanted to stay involved with things that were happening and be of assistance to everyone who took on my responsibilities at the bank."

Her lips tighten, unexpectedly, as she leans forward.

"I never wanted anyone to see that I was in pain or uncomfortable. I felt if I let them see that side of what was happening to me, I would destroy their confidence and hope for me. I always believed I would walk again and lead a productive life."

Yes, what she says makes sense—a quiet determination unclouded by self-pity. Is it right for me to bring up another subject, something perhaps not only uncomfortable, but inappropriate? Why not? Joyce is honest and open. She smiles as if she knows the next question. Okay, here it goes: What about the driver of the Jaguar? Did she know who piloted the potentially lethal machine that hit her? Was the woman drunk or under the influence of drugs? Did she ever make contact with Joyce?

She places a finger to her upper lip, a reflective pose. Surely, Joyce has strong opinions about the person who nearly killed her.

"No, I don't know who she was or why she hit me. I don't want to cause any further hurt in her life." Her tender smile seems incongruous. "I'm grateful that she stopped and called 911."

I didn't expect this kind of reaction to my question or to sense such a powerful benevolence. I needed to savor her words intellectually and emotionally rather than perfunctorily typed on a laptop. But there's more. Joyce's eyes forecast her words before they are spoken.

"I want to use my experience as a way to communicate a special message of hope to individuals who have suffered a traumatic event—whether physical, emotional, financial, or psychological." She raises her chin confidently, without arrogance. "And the message is that we all have it in us to deal with these tragedies and traumas, even if we don't believe that now. We all have it within us—we just need to use it when bad stuff happens." She grins, eyes twinkling. "I had a wonderful life before my accident and I have a wonderful life now."

Joyce has responded to every question without fanfare, pretense, or self-aggrandizement, just genuine, honest, and self-effacing answers. Enlightenment, inspiration, and admiration describe this first meeting, an extraordinary resilient and charming woman. As we say goodbye, a hearty handshake is replaced with a warm and sincere embrace. Joyce turns and walks towards her car parked far from the handicapped spots. Her gait is elegant and robust, a slight limp, almost imperceptible.

CHAPTER SIX

Co-Workers

TALL PINES AND BILLOWING OAKS absorb the late afternoon heat, a relief from the main road. I drive on an old Texas farm-to-market thoroughfare, transformed from a two-lane blacktop for tractors and pick-up trucks into a major artery for a Houston suburb, now citified with left turn lanes, traffic lights, and the city metro bus line. The usual hot and humid late April day seems cooler and dry to me thanks to a weak cold front from the northeast, but the trees comfort the tension caused by driving alongside delivery trucks, taxis, and harried commuters. Slowly, my clenched fingers, tightly grasping the steering wheel, begin to relax.

The condo building is called Timber Top and rightly so, rising eighteen stories between beautiful Ponderosa Pines, part of the Big Thicket's extension into northern Houston. Don, Joyce's significant other, opens the door followed by a friendly, natural smile. The condominium is on the twelfth floor overlooking two golf courses: Raveneaux and the internationally renowned Champions Golf Club, a spacious premier course created by Jack Burke and Jimmy Demaret in 1956, honored by hosting the Ryder Cup Matches in 1967 and the U.S. Open in 1969. Cleverly, the clubhouse was built so those dining at its restaurant could see the first and tenth tee boxes, the ninth and eighteenth greens, as well as the practice range—a designed course for tournaments so thousands of spectators could roam its grounds without ever venturing out on the playing field—a professional golfer's golf course.

This is the view from one of my windows where I currently live.
I am so fortunate to live on the twelfth floor in a high-rise
condominium overlooking two golf courses. I feel as if I am always
"outside," and being outdoors has always been a big part of my life.

The condo is clean and well appointed with comfortable furniture, functional lighting, and homey knickknacks, the décor stylish and well balanced reflecting Joyce's personality, an amalgam of classy tastes with no-nonsense Midwestern values. Her friends are sitting at a large living room table playing cards while talking and laughing, like a family of siblings during the holidays. Their greetings allay a strange feeling of intrusion, a party crasher who ingratiates his presence onto sacred family ground. No, no wine, diet coke only, caffeine to stimulate a mind on overload from the day's stresses. Food, healthy and home-cooked, sits atop the dining room table; these are caring people, and no matter what their lives are like or have been, Joyce's presence transcends all—family, not by blood, but by choice.

After introductions, we sit around the large opened coffee table, and slowly, their stories come forth.

"We decided to go to Joyce's house," Jennifer says, a co-worker at Klein Bank, now Amegy Bank. Joyce's fellow workers became concerned when she didn't show for a Friday morning meeting.

"Joyce is never late," Lynell says shaking her head. "We all started calling around to the other branches. Maybe she got mixed up." She gazes downward before looking up. "Everyone got worried."

"I called Jana," Connie says, eyes strained and serious.

Jana was Klein Bank's designated police officer used for security reasons, especially after a rash of bank robberies at their supermarket locations. After twenty years on the service, Jana knew when there was trouble.

Connie continues, "Jana was at the station booking an arrest when I called her and told her that Joyce hadn't shown up at work." Connie eyes widen. "She told me to send someone to Joyce's house to see if her car was there and, if not, then to go to Memorial Park."

Jennifer chimes in. "I went to her house thinking maybe she was sick. But when she didn't answer the door, I knew I had to go to the park and look for her car."

Lynell speaks next. "I told her she wasn't going to go by herself. 'Jennifer,' I said, 'Look, I have a gun and we're going together.'" They all laugh.

"We knew it was her car," Jennifer continues. "All her office papers were sitting on the back seat."

That was Joyce, they agreed—a workaholic.

Jennifer's voice becomes softer. "We asked the man at the tennis center if he knew anything about a missing runner. He paused before nodding and told us he thought he knew who we were looking for. 'Probably the person hit by a car earlier this morning,' he said solemnly." Jennifer wets her lips. "He told us that it was a bad accident." She swallows hard while the others remain quiet, some with bowed heads, others staring gravely at Jennifer, absorbing the story as if they were hearing it for the first time. "We knew it had to be Joyce. She never missed a meeting before."

All her fellow banking colleagues agreed; Joyce was efficient and punctual. No one had heard from her that morning and assumed Joyce was the victim. Later, they found out for sure. Lila, Joyce's very close friend who works at a different bank, identified her at Hermann Hospital trauma center.

*Many reasons and people made a big difference in my recovery:
my family, great doctors and medical facilities. The list is endless,
but eight very special people in my life were always with me
in body and mind from when I was in the Hermann Trauma Center
until this very day. These are people I work with, but they are more
than that—they are dear friends. They are, in the back row from left to
right: Jennifer Pittman, Naomi Kleb, Rhonda Krahn and Lynell Soltys.
In the front row: Diane Mangum, Peggy Coleman, myself,
Connie Taylor and Gloria Ewert.*

"Jana took me to see Joyce at the trauma center," Connie says. She pauses and takes a deep, pensive breath. "I'll never forget that moment when I knew it was Joyce lying there. Jana grabbed the collar of my business suit before I fainted." She stares upward, trying to regain composure. "Later, Jana said that even after twenty years as a police officer, she had never seen such a mangled body—swollen head, blood dripping from Joyce's eye sockets." Her voice fades and can't continue.

"I was a thousand miles away," Naomi says, her voice quivering slightly. "I just went back to my room and cried."

Till now, it was like a bunko party or a girls' night out. Laughter, hugging, simple talk—but Connie's and Naomi's comments hit a painful memory, something they'd forgotten about for several years. Connie leans her head back before speaking.

"There was no doubt in my mind that Joyce would survive." She gesticulates with both hands. "She was too strong, too confident, too much loved to die like this."

"We prayed and prayed," Naomi says. "We prayed at church, we prayed at work, we prayed at home."

"And now we're stronger," a comment from Peggy. All nod. Suddenly, Connie turns toward Don. "Don't you agree?"

Don hasn't said anything, pensively staring at his cupped hands. Slowly, he leans forward and adjusts his glasses. "Yes, absolutely," he says perfunctorily.

"Don was one of the first people I called when I found out about Joyce," Connie says while staring at him. "You weren't even dating Joyce anymore then, but I knew you needed to be included."

Don doesn't answer. He and Joyce broke up several months before the accident. While there's no anger in Connie's comment, one wonders what event or conflict caused the relationship to end. No answers will be discovered tonight; only that Don and Joyce became a couple again after the accident.

There is a sudden air of uneasiness among the group. Connie senses it. "Well, Joyce's accident made you two stronger, don't you think, Don?"

He nods without hesitation. "Yes, it did."

A simple response, but genuine; did he see Joyce differently after the accident? Was his love for her always there but rekindled by her near death? He didn't have to become re-involved during her hospitalization, nor with her long rehabilitation or adjustment to life; but he did, and their relationship has been solid ever since.

"Where is Peter?" someone asks.

"Oh, he called and he's on his way," Joyce says calmly. She sits near the window and smiles—a gentle smile, warm and considerate. She has listened to her friends without interruption, like a wise guru permitting students to explore their feelings without judgment. Her presence is not definable yet, a metaphysical uniqueness untarnished by human foibles. It is her inner strength that brings her friends into a state of equanimity with good karma; but where is Peter who agreed to attend tonight's meeting? Where is the boy/man who suddenly faced tough adult decisions at the age of twenty?

Jennifer shifts in her chair. "Peter and I had many talks when his mom was in a coma," she says, her smile now transformed into a taut gaze. "I don't know how he did it."

Peggy shakes her head. "I felt so sorry for Peter. Here is this young man with a two-month-old daughter, and now the doctors are asking him questions about resuscitation and organ transplants."

The room is silent. Don gets up and walks to the kitchen.

Joyce knows when to smile, an uncanny sense when people are feeling uncomfortable. "The nurses were great to Peter," she says. "I heard they brought a crib over so Ally could sleep while Peter stayed at the hospital."

Several laugh. "They were enamored with Ally," Lynell says. "They gave Peter a separate room and a crib they got from the pediatrics unit. The rest of us stayed in the conference room."

"We became friends with the staff," Connie says. "They never saw so many people come for one person."

The emotional air is lighter now. Joyce's friends are cheerful again. Amazingly, Joyce has brought them from unpleasant memories to a more tranquil presence, part of her many special talents; but what about Peter? Why isn't he here? Was he able to emotionally transcend those memories, times when his mother wasn't supposed to make it, let alone walk and return to work? How did he manage fathering and make critical decisions? How did he mentally maintain himself during his mother's surgeries, her infections, her rehabilitations?

As if on cue, the door opens and Peter walks in, a clean young face with a serious countenance, too serious for a twenty-six-year-old. Everyone greets him. He sits in a chair just outside the open living room, close enough to be seen, but strategically on the periphery. More talk about Joyce's accident, the hospital, her fractured spine, hip, and legs—Peter listens for several minutes, and then quietly goes out to the terrace to smoke. Intuitively, Gloria walks outside and talks to him. When he reenters the condo, he whispers in his mother's ear and leaves discreetly.

No one says anything about Peter after he's gone. More talk about Joyce, her work ethics, pleasant personality, and physical and emotional fortitude. It all goes into my laptop, uplifting comments and the group's interactions, a testimony to their camaraderie. It's a good feeling shared by all; but Peter is an enigma—his story, his feelings, and his memories remain hidden.

Chapter Seven

Lila's Notes

10-20-00
911 CALL AT 4:51 AM PER HOSPITAL.
Arrived Hermann trauma 5:35 AM—Dr. Red Duke trauma team.

Dr. Duke asked me if I knew why it took so long to get her to them.

Jogging on 1000 block of 610 feeder road—in street-construction—Don has pictures. Jaguar struck Joyce at fifty miles an hour, she landed on Jag and broke windshield, was thrown one hundred and twenty feet in front of Jag and car ran over left side. Speed limit thirty-five.

Joyce missed a 7:00 A.M. meeting, 10:00 A.M. meeting and luncheon. Connie, one of her Branch administrators called me at 2:30 and asked me to meet police at her house to see if she was home. Couldn't locate Peter or Tiffany. Police require family member to enter house; I'll tell them I'm her sister. Left my office, calling Lynell and telling them where a key was hidden so they wouldn't have to wait for me. Joyce is missing.

I asked someone to go to the park and look for her car; Jennifer and Lynell went to Memorial Park and found her car. Park office had note from Hermann Neuro-Trauma if anyone missing calls as they had a Jane Doe jogger. I went to her house and waiting for sheriff, jumped the back fence and her car wasn't in garage.

Called Rhonda at bank—she gave number of Cindy—social worker at hospital provided by Jennifer. I called and she told me where to meet her at hospital—stayed on the phone with me guiding me into the medical center as traffic was heavy.

My dear friend of many years, Lila Hamman. Lila identified me at Hermann Hospital when I was "Jane Doe" and was by my side physically and mentally throughout my stay at Hermann and remains a wonderful person in my life.

Met Cindy and a doctor at the ER section of the hospital. Cindy walked with me to the trauma conference room and asked me if I could describe Joyce, early fifties, long hair, petite, greenish eyes, had long slender tapered hands. Remembered Joyce had told me she had done something "wild" to her fingernails and was getting a kick out of reactions from staff, etc. Would show me when she came over to see my family. Clothes: running shorts, tank top, would be wearing a black fanny pack; no she didn't carry ID in it, just wore it to pick up coins, would probably be empty if she was running in the dark.

Cindy asked me to wait and left her tablet on the table. It contained the EMT report and I called Rhonda and asked her to quickly type down what I was reading, which she did. Cindy came back into the room and suggested I come with her to see the Jane Doe.

We went up a flight of back stairs into a Neuro-trauma unit; she asked me to remain outside. She came back and walked me to the bed at the far left side of the unit. I saw this very large person on a burgundy rubber mattress, with most of her body covered.

It looked like the Michelin Man or something from outer space on the bed. I saw Dr. Red Duke at the head of the bed and probably eight or more doctors stepped back.

I couldn't accept this was Joyce but found a piece of her hair at the back of her neck support and it was Joyce's very tightly curled hair, I found one of her hands and saw it bruised and swollen, but definitely Joyce's once slender fingers with "silver metallic" nail polish. Her eyes were closed and the right side of her face and eye socket were crushed and grotesque. She had a large hole in the side of her head. Her closed eyes were filled with pooled blood and yellow liquids and her entire tongue was extended out of her mouth, her face was the size of a large dinner plate, but the distorted features were definitely Joyce's.

I said "This is Joyce, she is training for her twenty-fourth marathon and I've never known her to quit on anything important. She is fifty-two years old, in excellent condition, and the only thing I've known her to have was back surgery. She was running six weeks after surgery. Joyce is very disciplined and if she has a mind, she'll will her body to live and heal. If you question whether to go forward or hold on treatment—GO!—she will fight with you and never give up if she has a brain left to process. She has an unbelievable threshold for pain and endurance. She is from Minnesota dairy country and has run with armed escorts in The Honduras."

All kinds of alarms went off and Cindy led me out of the room. But I leaned down and said "Joyce, it's Lila. Hold on, I know you're going to make it, just stay with us, we need you, Peter needs you." As I turned to walk away, I realized my feet were soaked with red fluids that had been running off the side of the bed.

CHAPTER EIGHT

Meeting Lila

NEATNESS TRANSFORMED INTO CHAOS. Furniture, once in perfect symmetry with the condo's decor, is now turned every which way with stuffed animals, toys, and games strewn throughout the living room. Joyce's grandchildren, Ally five and Clay three, greet me, a total stranger, with cautious smiles.

"Say hello," Joyce commands in a smooth, reassuring voice.

They're both adorable and it's easy to feel their love for Grandma.

Joyce turns, her happy face and mannerisms reveal no apology.

"Tiffany and the kids were visiting. They're about to leave."

It's easy to talk with them. Children's innocence is special, an ethereal gift to be cherished. Tiffany appears from another room. She's tall with natural beauty; her handshake exudes confidence.

"Nice to meet you. We're just leaving."

It's odd, an ex-daughter-in-law's friendship with her children's grandmother; but should it be odd? They're all family; divorce doesn't have to include everyone else. Why did she and Peter break up? Was it a relationship problem, or did Joyce's accident create insurmountable stress, enough to sever a love, if it existed at all?

"Bye, Grandma!" they each yell. Their tender, sweet hugs are endearing.

Several minutes later, the doorbell rings.

"That's Lila," Joyce says smiling. Everyone has confirmed their friendship—long and lasting—but what kind of woman is she?

They hug in the foyer, faces camouflaged by paintings and mirrors from the wall.

"I'd like you to meet Lila," Joyce says, her arm tenderly wrapped over her friend's shoulder.

Lila's smile appears restrained, and suddenly, it's like the first time at Joyce's place—the feeling that I'm a guest no one really knows. After pleasantries, Lila and I sink into big comfortable chairs, but Joyce sits upright in a straight-back chair; is it a reflection of her past when a pedantic teacher in a one-room, rural Minnesota school house demanded obedience, as well as posture, from her students?

Surprisingly, Lila takes charge and asks a question, direct and important.

"Why are you interested in Joyce's accident?" Her facial features speak defiance, but the sudden sheepish grin says, I'm sorry to be so forward. While Lila's emotions have not been discounted, their impact may have been underestimated. Quietly, but without submission, I answer her question: to create an account, without sensationalism, about Joyce's survival, her unbreakable courage and resilient optimism; her life was not only disrupted, but her passion to run, perhaps to walk, was in jeopardy.

Lila rubs her forehead pensively. When she looks up, she smiles—this time with genuine friendliness.

"I needed to know. And honestly, I have been trying to avoid you."

Laughter, but it's out of politeness rather than relief. Something is disturbing Lila. Unexpected, she wipes her tears.

"I didn't realize how much I was suppressing," she says, although her voice barely cracks. "Joyce is my best friend and I was going through some tough times before the accident." She sips her water. "And Joyce was my confidant and my support. Now," she says and pauses; "now she was in a coma."

Silence while gathering thoughts. Surely, a trauma like the one Joyce sustained affected all who knew and loved her; but the impact on Lila was particularly intense and the reasons for this come quickly. Recently separated from her boyfriend, Lila was now living with her daughter. Stressed, unnerved, and confused, she turned to Joyce, the two having shared emotions when they both went through their divorces.

"She was the only one who understood what I was feeling." She swallows hard before continuing. "I would call her two, three times a day." She turns toward Joyce and smiles. Her friend reciprocates with a gentle turning of her head, a gesture of understanding, empathy, and love.

Lila leans back and raises her chin reflectively. I was at work when they called me from the bank. The first thing I thought was that Joyce was attacked during her run." She grins and shakes her head. "I was so angry at you," she says to Joyce. "I told you a hundred times not to run without an ID."

Joyce nods deliberately like a great master whose disciple has had an epiphany, a profound understanding of a deep concept, introspective and edifying. There is no pretense in Joyce's gesture, but a genuine acknowledgment and affirmation, the kind that emanates from those who are at peace with themselves. Joyce gets up, but instead of walking over to Lila, she heads for the kitchen.

"I drove over to her house," Lila continues. "I knew if her car wasn't in the garage, she never made it back from the park." Lila takes a long drink and looks up, eyes intense with tightened lips. "Joyce's friends at work called the sheriff's department, but heck, I wasn't going to wait for them. My son called me on my cell and told me not to go into the house. I guess he was afraid I would find Joyce murdered or something else terrible, but I wasn't scared."

Lila's voice is deliberately articulate, every word rolling off her tongue with precision, her soft South Texas accent almost imperceptible.

"I leaped over the fence into Joyce's backyard. I knew the door would be unlocked." She smiles. "Peter and she never locked doors, another thing that bothered me."

Their nexus is obvious—a friendship fundamentally based on acceptance, two women connecting emotionally.

Lila and I with my two "pals," Connor and Theo. Connor and Theo are miniature Pomeranians and definitely lighten up my life.

She takes a deep breath. "Her car wasn't there and I knew she'd never come home. I left and headed for the park."

"Where was Peter?" I ask. "Why wasn't he home?" Lila explains that he was at Tiffany's place, helping with the new baby.

"I called Jennifer at the bank, but she and Lynell had already left for the park. We all knew by now that something had happened to her." She swallows. "When they called me and told me about the Jane Doe at Hermann Hospital, I didn't know how to feel; glad that she was alive, but frightened about the extent of her injuries." She shifts in her chair. "They told me that the hospital could only release information to family, so I said 'just tell them I'm her sister!'" Her smile evaporates almost instantaneously. "Cindy, a hospital social worker who deals with unidentified victims, called me on my cell. I gave her Joyce's description, her height, weight, hair color, and age, but she said it didn't match." Her grin returns. "She said Jane Doe was in her late thirties and had curly hair, not a woman in her fifties with long silky hair." She takes another sip. "But the accident occurred around the time Joyce would have been at the park, so she told me to come to the hospital anyway." Lila laughs. "None of us knew that Joyce had curly hair. She straightened it, but when she ran, the sweat and humidity made it curl."

Joyce comes back with a tray of crackers, cheese, and fresh fruit, a simple presentation on small elegant plates. She sits down with perfect posture and places a piece of cheddar on a tiny cracker delicately. "These are healthy for you, made of seven grains."

Lila leans back and laughs. "Joyce, what difference does it make as long as it tastes good?"

Joyce raises her hand, long feminine fingers manicured with a classy gloss. Her gestures match her speech and especially her persona—sophisticated, stylish, and warm. "Lila, you know I eat healthy. Always have and always will."

Lila grins and shakes her head. She doesn't have to say anything. She knows her friend, her likes and dislikes, her quirks and idiosyncrasies, as well as her strengths and endearing personality traits. No words are needed.

Lila turns and her loving gaze transforms into a stern countenance—more about Joyce's accident.

"Anyway, Cindy, the social worker, told me to come to the hospital to identify the Jane Doe. The traffic was terrible, Friday rush hour and a huge back up on I-10. I called Cindy back and she talked me through downtown and out onto 288 to the back of the Medical Center. I would have lost it without her help."

Lila places some cheese on a seven grain cracker and chews it slowly—a momentary break, a quick respite from her thoughts.

"Cindy had me park in some reserved spot and met me at the Emergency Room trauma center. She took me to a room and had me sign some papers. I wanted to tell her that I wasn't Joyce's sister—I don't like lying—but I knew I had to for Joyce's sake." She sighs. "They brought in her running shorts and top." She pauses and looks up. "It was Joyce's," she says softly. Lila sits up in her chair as the memories return, strong and painful, as intense as the time it happened. She stares at her hands.

"Cindy took me into the trauma room where they were working on Joyce." She wets her lips. "There must have been ten doctors around her bed. Tubes and machines everywhere; water and blood on the floor." She looks up with a slight smile. "You know, I just remembered what I thought when I saw Joyce. You couldn't see her face or her body since she was wrapped in some kind of strange plastic thing that either had air or water circulating in it—the Michelin Man."

I bolt upright in the cushiony chair. "What? The Michelin Man?" I ask incredulously. Even Joyce narrows her eyes.

"I know it sounds crazy, but that's what my eyes saw—the Michelin Man—you know, the character they use for Michelin Tires—the guy who is made up of tires—that's what Joyce looked like." She shakes her head. "Weird, huh? I hadn't thought about it since that day."

There's silence while three people try to make sense of this observation. Is it funny, a comic relief? Or is it sad that Joyce, once fit and healthy, now resembled an advertising caricature, a man with tires for a body?

Lila leans back. "Then I saw her hands." She looks up, her face slightly distorted, fingers twisted tight. "How could I not know Joyce's hands? Long fingers, smooth skin, so feminine and unique." She swallows and looks up, tears welling in her eyes. "Her nails. Joyce told me a few days before that she did something wild with her nails and would show me that weekend. Metallic. Couldn't believe it—conservative Joyce having metallic sparkling glitter on her nails!"

Lila wipes her eyes as Joyce gestures with an understanding nod.

"He must have seen me," Lila continues. "Dr. Red Duke. He yelled something at me."

A Houston icon, the tall, gruff, country-talking trauma surgeon with the thick handlebar moustache was heading the realm that Friday at the Hermann Hospital ER. His tough persona hid a tender heart, a man who gave back to the community, especially to school children, giving talks about health and medicine; but under fire, he was a hot pistol, a metaphor perfect for his central Texas roots. A product of Dallas' Parkland Hospital training, he was a resident in the ER when President Kennedy was shot and brought in.

"'Do you know her?' he screamed at me." Lila takes a deep breath. "'Yes, she's a marathon runner,' I yelled back to him. He moved towards me, away from Joyce's gurney. 'How old is she,' he asked, leaning his face close to mine. I said, 'She's fifty-two, and if she still has a mind, she needs to live.' I remember him straightening up and rubbing his chin. 'Well, hell, if she's in that good shape, maybe she will.' He moved back to the bed. I didn't know what to think." Lila shakes her head. "I just stared at the Michelin Man knowing that Joyce's body and spirit were in there." She swallows. "That's when I heard the alarm." Lila bit her lower lip. "The heart monitor—it went flat on the screen. A doctor jumped on the bed and began pounding her chest. That's when Dr. Duke ordered me to get out. All I remember is Cindy pulling my arm and taking me out of the trauma room. My feet felt wet and I looked at my shoes." She swallows hard. "I was standing in a pool of blood."

CHAPTER NINE

Don

I HAVE KNOWN JOYCE FOR ABOUT FIFTEEN YEARS. We ran together in Memorial Park from nineteen ninety till the spring of two thousand. We ran marathons together, both locally and at various locations around the U.S. We had a personal relationship during this period. I have always admired Joyce for her ability to live and act in the present. This contrasts with my tendency to think too much (worry).

We were no longer in a relationship on October 20, 2000 when I received a phone call at work from a mutual friend. She told me that Joyce had been in an accident. I went immediately to the trauma center at Hermann Hospital to see how she was. Many of her friends and banking associates were already there. It was questionable whether Joyce would survive. I was able to see her for a few minutes in the ICU. We were informed that the next seventy-two hours were critical. If Joyce survived that, then she would probably live in spite of her extensive injuries.

I visited the hospital on each of the next few days and kept in touch with mutual friends during the rest of the critical period. Also, I visited Joyce a few times while she remained at the Hermann Trauma Center. She was always unconscious during these visits.

When Joyce was transferred to Beacon Rehabilitation, I visited her there as well. It was very difficult to see her being tortured by all those medical devices. Nevertheless, Joyce always seemed upbeat. I never saw her in a bad mood or feeling sorry for herself. The rehab seemed to last forever.

After Joyce was out of Beacon, I didn't see her again until she moved into her new house with Peter and her granddaughter. I visited and sometimes took Joyce out to dinner. I also accompanied Joyce to some bank-related functions. Eventually, we renewed our relationship.

I know that Joyce always assumed she would recover from her injuries. I think I did too. Having seen her deal with whatever came along, I just knew she would handle this as well. True to form, her recovery has been miraculous.

Since the Beacon Rehabilitation was in the bank's business area, it was possible for her to participate in business from her bed. I think this was an enormous advantage to her recovery.

I know that when the accident occurred, Joyce was running a twenty-miler, practicing for a marathon. We had run this route together many times. We usually ran along that feeder from south to north with our backs to the traffic. It always felt dangerous, even on Sundays when we did our long runs. This was a Friday when the traffic was heavier. Joyce had told me that she was running this route in the other direction, to get that part along the feeder done early and to do it facing traffic. It's a mystery to me how she got hit when she was facing traffic. The bridge that she was on had no sidewalk and it had two lanes.

Don Larson and Joyce. Don and I began as running buddies and then dated for many years. For a time we did not see each other and then "fell in love" again. Don is the love of my life and my soul mate.

CHAPTER TEN

Al Jeter, RN

"SHE WAS A TRAIN WRECK, A REAL TRAIN WRECK. Over ninety percent of her bones were broken."

Friendly and generous with a big smile—that's the best way to describe Al Jeter, a nurse working at Beacon Rehabilitation Hospital, now called Nexus Specialty Hospital.

"Let me show you her room," Al says, walking quickly through the corridors across squeaky-clean white linoleum floors. Surprisingly, the place doesn't smell like a hospital, nothing one would expect in a chronic care facility built over ten years ago for head injury patients. Where are the annoying urine and fecal scents that permeate most medical facilities? Why is this place so spic-and-span clean? And the peripheral noise—hardly a sound—no overhead loudspeakers, no incessant chirping from heart monitors, and no radio or TV noise. Library atmosphere would be stretching it, but calmness and quietude prevail, a contrast to a typical medical unit.

"Man, she was in bad shape when she got here," Al continues. "I mean, broken back, arms, legs, knees, and then all that hardware." He gestures to his head. "That halo, neck, it was screwed into her skull. Then the rods and plates, and the external fixator. Geez!"

While it's the first floor, Joyce's room is numbered three-thirteen. Maybe this time, that number was lucky. The room is vacant.

"Yep, this is her place. I was the night nurse on duty, twelve-hour shift, seven P.M. till seven A.M."

The room is small, but the bed is complex, an instrument used to maneuver the crippled or the brain-damaged patient. There is little light from the outside, unlike Joyce's current panoramic window views of golf courses from her high-rise. How could a conscious person, unable to move, tied down by bulky metal, an indwelling bladder catheter, and a heavy head-band screwed into her skull, not become depressed and withdrawn, particularly in a dark hole like this? Maybe Joyce insisted on being moved to the hallway, where the sharp fluorescent lighting and shiny white walls would brighten her spirits; or maybe outdoors, if feasible, where she could gaze at the green foliage and smell nature's invigorating ambrosia. Surely they did this for her.

"I'm telling you, she was something," Al continues. "What a woman." He looks contemplative. "I know she must have been down, but she never showed or said it."

The twenty-bed chronic care facility, established by Dr. John Cassidy in nineteen ninety-five to house brain-injured patients, is located in The Woodlands, Texas, a master planned community located about thirty miles north of Houston. Nestled within the tall pines of the Big Thicket, a national preserve consisting of several ecosystems including eastern hardwood forests, Gulf coastal plains, and Midwestern prairies, The Woodlands offers residents one hundred forty-five miles of hike and bike trails, over one hundred parks including ponds, lakes, swimming pools, a waterway meandering through its town center, and championship golf courses. While some refer to its strict zoning and bureaucratic community association rules as "Disneywoods," The Woodlands rivals downtown Houston with the finest restaurants, shopping, and entertainment amenities. Joyce didn't choose this paradise, an oasis within a large urban quagmire; fortunately, Beacon was a rehab facility covered by her insurance company and easily accessible by her friends and, especially, Peter. More importantly, her care was exceptional.

Al throws open the doors to a larger room, a bizarre scene consisting of an odd-shaped bathtub raised above the ground by a pulley mechanism, a kind of tub on an elevator.

"This is where she received her whirlpool treatments," Al says proudly.

While the room seems innocuous, Joyce experienced agonizing pain when placed on a "slab" and transported to the water treatments for wound cleaning, usually with a narcotic pretreatment required. Suddenly, the room gives an aura of medieval horror; is this what Don referred to as torture?

Al is busy and must go back to his charting. He shakes his head before saying goodbye. "I tell you, she's a remarkable woman." He laughs. "You know, three days after being here, I swear, this person, who was close to being dead a few weeks before, now covered in metal like the tin man, with a gaping, oozing wound from her emergency abdominal incision, tied to rods and hooks, unable to move any extremity, with most of her body crushed, began doing bank business on her laptop."

"What?" I ask skeptically. "I know she did some work from Beacon, but not three days after her arrival."

Al smiles and shakes his head. "Yep, it was crazy," he continues, "she pushed her bedside call button more for help with setting up her computer and cell phone than she did for pain medication."

He stares at the shiny floor for a few moments before looking up. "Hey, tell her hello for me. She's one in a million."

CHAPTER ELEVEN

Convincing Peter

PETER,

I have read the first forty pages of the book and I like how they are written—not gory or lots of pain, etc. I can bring them to you if you would like. I'm not forcing you or asking you to speak to Randy, but based on talking to everyone else, he realizes what an amazing and wonderful part you played in helping me recover. I look back and realize I was so busy trying to make sure we had enough money to live on; but my accident gave me a second chance to have a wonderful relationship with you and your children.

I will be in Comfort, Texas starting Friday afternoon through Sunday, but will talk to you when I get back. When I first met with Randy, I told him I did not want this to be about me, the marathon runner who got run over. I wanted to help other people realize that bad stuff happens, and we don't think we have it within us to deal with it, but we do. I also told him that I did not want anything negative to be said about the woman that hit me. She did call 911 and that saved my life. He has agreed.

This is something that I want to do for others, and you were such a big part of my will to live and recover. I remember when you took care of me when I left Beacon. You had the baby monitor on me so I could call you when I needed to get up during the night. I remember when you asked me if I could drink less before I went to bed, so I wouldn't get up so many times. Finally I learned how to sleep with my tennis shoes on so I could get up myself.

I remember when the home health care nurse came and how you learned to take care of my skin grafts, and when you built my bathtub seat so I could take a shower, and the "sliding board." It was my way to get from one place to another. I remember being on the living room sofa and you would have to do a muscle man lift to get me up, and you asked me if I was gaining weight!

I remember you taking me to the doctors after the flood and all of the tunnels were unavailable. Ally would sit on my lap, like an unmoving doll, and you would push me. Remember when we got stuck in the grates and how hard we laughed?

And then all of the trips to physical therapy which were at Ally's nap time. She and you were very patient.

And finally I decided to go to work while I was in my wheelchair and you drove me every day and picked me up. When I felt that I could drive myself, you were doubtful but supportive, and rode with me for a week or so before following me to work in your car to make sure I got there. I called you when I was leaving work and you were always sitting on the steps when I got home.

I remember you rushing home when I had food poisoning. You were always there then and are always there now. That is what your involvement in the book is about. I could not have made it without you. You gave me a reason to live. I want to give that reason to others along with the confidence that we may not think we can do it when stuff gets bad, but we all have it within us to do so if we choose.

Everyone that has talked to Randy has been so complimentary and impressed at the decisions and support that you gave me since the accident and after. They are amazed at "what you had to manage" at twenty-one years old. Let him meet you and your girlfriend Meghan. I think the talk will be good for you and her. You gave me a reason to live and helped me to regain a wonderful life with you and your children. Now I want to help others.

Lots of love,
Mom

*

RANDY,

I spoke to Peter and he is adamant that I be present. It has taken me the better part of six months to get him to agree to talk about this. This whole situation is very emotional and depressing for him. We will have the kids this weekend, but we can meet you at Joyce's condo on Saturday around three, if that is okay with you. Peter doesn't want Joyce to be there, and I hope you can understand that. She will be out of town this weekend, but we have a key to the house. Let me know if this time works for you, or if you have another time that would be more convenient. Starbucks does sound good, but I don't believe the kids would be too pleased about a coffee shop. Thank you for all of your understanding, and working with me on this. Hope to hear from you soon.

Regards,
Meghan

Peter and Meghan whom I love dearly.

CHAPTER TWELVE

Meeting Peter

ALLY AND CLAY ANSWER THE DOOR, excited to be at Grandma's house with their dad and his girlfriend sans Grandma. Their smiles exude happiness and security. While their mom and dad are divorced, parental love is obvious. Having them here mitigates some of my anxiousness created by meeting Peter, the boy/man commended by all who know Joyce; but why his reticence? Is he uncomfortable sharing his mother's life or, perhaps, something deeper? I sense that "uninvited guest" feeling, a stranger crashing a family event.

It's the living room with the panoramic views of the golf courses, only this time, the curtains are closed and the bright sunlight streams through a sliver of window, an eye-squinting blazing glare. Peter sits in the same chair Lila had occupied, only this time my view is from a seat further away, the glowing daylight like a police detective's hotspot on me, the suspect. He is in command, this is his domain, or at least his mother's house without her presence. A kid's show is blaring from the TV, just to the left. No cheese, crackers, or fruit this time—just Peter, his children, and his girlfriend—and me, an outsider who must seem insolent and annoying. The whine of the laptop is utterly indefensible, an enemy in the wrong camp. Even the soy latte has lost its warmth.

"I want you to know that I'm doing this for my mother."

I nod in acknowledgment. "But why?" I ask.

Peter leans back in his chair. His shaved head contrasts with the photo on the table behind him, a handsome young man in a tux, a full head of hair with a broad, friendly smile. Before the accident? Before his divorce? Doesn't matter—he is Joyce's only child, and while the reception is chilly and borders on anger, there is kindness in his face, especially when Clay, who precociously senses his dad's unrest, climbs onto Peter's lap. Tenderly, Peter kisses his son's head and hugs him with genuine caresses. Peter's façade has been broken by a three-year-old.

"I know my mom wants me to talk with you, so go ahead. Ask me what you want to."

The TV noise competes with the interaction. I relate his mother's comment, that she could not have picked a better son off the shelf, which elicits a grin.

"She always put me on a pedestal," he answers apathetically. He leans forward. Clay gets down and runs into the kitchen to play with his sister and Meghan, Peter's girlfriend. "I'm not proud of myself."

What? Not proud? The son who made grown-up decisions when his mother was critically ill is ashamed? "Of what?"

"I was drunk the whole time. Morning, daytime, nighttime," he says nonchalantly. He leans back, smile gone. "It was the only way I could get by."

The brutal honesty is unexpected. Suddenly, Peter, through his own disclosure, is not the pure shining knight as advertised; but he made good decisions, intelligent ones based on strong personal beliefs and his mother's tenets. How drunk could he have been and why is he admitting it? He rubs his bald head, a little harder than the soft touches he used with Clay, and stares at the floor.

"You know, it isn't easy to talk about this." He looks up, this time with a vulnerable stare, the angry persona shed. "The night I came here, when you and all my mom's friends were here, well, I didn't think it would be a big deal, but it was and I couldn't talk." He shakes his head. "I went out to the balcony and just cried."

My cold latte goes down with a hard swallow. My assumption that Peter wasn't interested in talking and spent the hour on the balcony smoking was wrong, dead wrong. He was re-grieving his mother's accident, and perhaps, his own guilt. Why wasn't that obvious to me—a son and his mother—a relationship untouched by divorce—stronger than any bond, now threatened. He was scared out of his wits, and a phony bravado, created by male machismo, hid his fear.

"Let me start from the beginning," he offers. Suddenly, Peter's relaxed and cooperative. "I got a call from Jennifer telling me that Mom had been in an accident while running at Memorial Park. It didn't really faze me then, you know, about the seriousness of it all, but Jennifer sounded all upset." He clasps his hands in a reflective pose. "I still didn't get it. I mean, yeah, Mom was in an accident, but I knew she was strong." He smiles, "Hell, she'd run twenty-plus marathons by now." Slowly, he shakes his head. "I never ever thought about her dying."

Peter is silent for a few seconds, either trying to remember details, but more likely to gain composure. He may seem tough, but he's full of feelings, deep vulnerable ones.

"I went to the hospital with Ally and Jennifer. There were a bunch of people there, all of Mom's bank friends. Oh, and Don, Don was there also."

Why? Don wasn't in Joyce's life at that time. Did Peter know why, or was his mother just private about her relationships?

"I don't know who called Don, but he was there. My mom's friends and bank people had always been kept separate from me." He smiles again. "My mom and I are and have been tight, so her social life was hers and mine was mine."

Separate? Why did Joyce maintain two different worlds—her life on the outside and her life with Peter—over-protective, or insulating her only child from others and the harshness of life? No, Peter had a child and significant other. Obviously, they knew about each other's social existence. Insightfully, Peter senses the questions.

"You got to understand, my mom and I are like one." He grins sheepishly. "Yeah, I was a spoiled brat. Everything was done for me. Guess my mom mothered me too much." He stretches his arms. "But I took care of her as well." Another grin. "I didn't like Don at first, you know, he was dating my mom. But hell, it was her life anyway. She could do whatever she wanted as long as it didn't include me."

So many conditions, but it worked for them, each taking care of the other without disturbing their relationships. Perhaps, the divorce created a need for isolation; Joyce's pain from a broken marriage, Peter's loss of his father.

"Yeah, well, I like Don now. He's all right. Doesn't bother me. He's quiet and hell, it's my mom's business anyway, not mine."

Peter gulps a Coke. "Anyway, I didn't know how bad my mom was hurt until the doctor sat down with all of us in the conference room at the trauma center." His calm facial features contrast with a disturbing stare. "When he told us about all her injuries and that she might not live, we all started crying. All of us, including Don."

A room full of people affected by Joyce's accident because they loved her. Friend, lover, or child—she inspired all who knew her—her equanimity, geniality, and magnanimity unparalleled. And Matthew Sultemeier, the EMS who witnessed a near death accident victim moving her legs in a valiant, unconscious attempt to undo injuries, a maimed victim with an unquenchable desire to survive, called Joyce "a very special woman."

Meghan comes into the living room with Ally and Clay who sit near the TV, pick up crayons, and draw in their coloring books. She has kept them busy, while not excluding them. Sensitive to adult issues, they recognize the gravity of the conversation and want to be closer to their dad.

"The doctors let me see Mom a few hours later; I guess after they resuscitated her." He shakes his head in disbelief, probably the same way he did when he saw his mother. "You know, Lila said Mom looked like the Michelin Man, but all I remember is that her head," he pauses as he recalls the scene, "her head, well, it was huge." His arms spread out widely like the proverbial fish story, his eyes glued to the floor. "I know this sounds crazy, but I thought about a Garbage Pail Kid, what was her name?" He rubs his forehead. "Oh yeah, Brainy Janie. Yeah, that was it, Brainy Janie," he says with a timid grin.

The Michelin man and a Garbage Pail Kid? But how else could Lila and Peter explain Joyce's transformation from a healthy, fit, and robust fifty-two-year-old woman to a "thing" bloated from swollen subcutaneous tissue? A kind of cellular scream, a response caused when Joyce's organs were damaged, created a greatly disrupted fluid balance as well as metabolic chaos. Her bones, once the foundation of her body, were broken; over ninety percent of her skeletal frame was surrounded by soft tissue contusions, a kind of total body trauma, now wrapped up in a billowing body-suit that compressed and heated congested flesh and bones, hence images of the Michelin man and Brainy Janie.

"You couldn't recognize her," Peter says solemnly.

Ally and Clay seem oblivious to his description. What has he told them about Grandma, and could they even comprehend it at their tender ages? Probably not, but intuitively, they must sense their father's emotions. They continue to draw. Peter sighs. He has purged terrible memories, but continues without further prompting.

"It was crazy those first few days. I didn't know these people and I never saw Don after that first night. Jennifer, Ally, and I slept on the hard conference room floor. The doctors said that the next seventy-two hours would be the most critical." He looks up, wide eyes revealing the confusion he felt then, at a time that his mother, his stalwart friend and parent, might die at any moment. "I called my dad," he says innocently. "I needed family."

Surprising, his father, a non-issue till now, is in the picture; and yet, Peter's reference to family makes sense. Overwhelmed with his mother's dire condition and unaccustomed to being with his mother's friends, he turned to his father, family.

"My dad understood. He immediately got on a train from Florida. He was here in three days." Peter smiles. "He's afraid of flying."

Something new again. The reasons for his parents' divorce, an unknown, takes on new light. His dad is neither a low-life nor a dead-beat, but a man who responded to his son's plea for help; perhaps, a concern for Joyce, a woman who was his high school sweetheart and wife.

Peter swigs more Coke. "My dad was great. He stayed with me for three weeks. Helped me out a lot. We talked and he gave me advice." Peter shakes his head. "I would have gone nuts without him here." Peter raises his chin while still staring at the floor. "He cooked for me and took care of the house. And we talked, talked a lot. It felt good."

How interesting to hear about his father, without anger or bitterness. Obviously, their relationship is a good one, trusting and caring. While a mother's love is essential, a father's nurturing complements the child's emotional rearing.

Meghan brings cookies for Ally and Clay and they thank her politely. Suddenly, as an afterthought, she turns the TV volume down.

"Everything was crazy those first few days, even after we knew my mom was going to live; but it didn't feel right, I mean, not about my mom's injuries, but about Lila running the show."

Whoa, a new wrinkle. Lila running the show? Why was Peter upset with his mother's best friend?

"She told everyone what to do, including me." He tightens his lips, a pensive look. "I guess my mom and Lila are a lot alike, maybe that's why they're best friends. You know, strong personalities, kind of no-nonsense people. Well, I didn't like her telling me what to do. So I asked my Dad, and he said that I needed to do what was best for me and my mom, and if I didn't, I might regret it for the rest of my life."

Sage fatherly advice. At twenty-one, and overly protected by his mother, Peter was ready to hear this; but it had to come from a man, a family person, preferably his dad, who basically told him to grow up, get a grip on his life, and don't let anyone tell him how to live.

Peter's natural smile resurfaces. "So I told Lila I was going to make the decisions, not her. Hell, she was pissed, so much so that she called my grandfather and told him to talk to me." He sighs. "Well, maybe she smelled the alcohol on my breath and was worried that I'd screw things up." He leans forward in an awkward and uncomfortable way. "Damn, my grandfather called me and told me that it was his daughter's life that I was dealing with." He looks up, eyes clear and determined. "I didn't need that from him. I needed encouragements, not threats." He shakes his head. "That one hurt. And that's why I don't like to talk to him anymore."

More purging. From reticence to gregariousness. The air-conditioner kicks in and a wave of cool air penetrates the indoor heat.

"Jennifer and Connie were real helpful. And Dr. Lilly, a neurologist; he told me to take Mom to Beacon." Peter pauses reflectively. "He was good too. Gave me sound advice."

Peter was taking over, slowly, and in his own way; but it must have been scary.

"You know," he says with his trademark grin, "I needed to grow up. My mom took care of everything, but now, I needed to look at the bank statements and all that. Damn, I've never done that before. And Mom's records were confusing. Rent, bills, all that stuff. My dad helped me at first, but then, he had to go back to Florida." Delicately, he clasps his hands. "But I figured it out."

"I visited Mom as much as possible when she was transferred to Beacon, but I needed some sanity, so I went back to my work as a carpenter."

Meghan is scolding Clay for something. Peter ignores it.

"I remember talking to my mom at Beacon. I'd told her about the accident and her injuries before, but I think this time she understood." He leans back and smiles. "She told me to get her clothes and that she was getting out of here." His smile broadens. "I knew she was getting better."

Peter stands and stretches. Is it a signal to leave, the end of the meeting? No, he sits down again. More to come.

"It was pretty awful for her at Beacon. Sometimes, I heard her screaming during the treatments. You got to understand my mom, she never rested, always moving, always doing something. Now she couldn't move her legs or her right arm, only her left hand." He laughs. "Damn, she could use her cell phone real well with that hand." He looks up with a smirk. "Hell, I think the cell phone is part of her body anyway."

Ally and Clay are tired of coloring and go back into the kitchen. Meghan has been good with them.

"I remember the first time my mom tried to stand. It was a big moment for her. After all those months, this was her test, something she talked about. And if she could stand, then she was closer to getting out, going home, and going back to work, although she was conferencing with the bank all day and working her laptop with her left fingers practically all night." Another smirk appears. "Hey, my mom grew up on a pig farm and baled hay. She likes to work." He pauses as his mouth tightens. "It didn't go well. The nurses and therapist held her without the support of her bed behind her. She fell backwards, almost immediately, and they caught her." He sighs and swallows. "Damn, she cried all night about it. I'd never seen her depressed before. It really tore me up."

This time it's Ally who goes to her dad. She pulls at his shirt to get his attention, and asks him if she can change the TV channel. Peter gives her permission, but it was probably a ploy to take her dad away from unpleasant thoughts.

"Anyway, that wasn't a good day, but eventually, she was able to stand, and slowly, was able to take steps. She was always on me about going home. She drove the doctors and staff crazy, constantly bugging them about going home. She'd tell them that I could take care of her better than anyone." He shakes his head. "I wasn't sure."

Something else is bothering him. No doubt, caring for his mom at home would be challenging, but there's more. After a few moments of silence, it becomes apparent.

"Tiffany and I weren't getting along well. She didn't want my mom to come home. Said it would be better for her to go to some kind of place where she'd get better care." Peter takes a deep breath. "But my mom wanted to come home. So, the night before I brought her back, Tiffany moved out with Ally."

Ouch, an unenviable dilemma, a conflict irresolvable and without compromise. Mother versus significant other and child. But should I ask him? Now I felt more comfortable with Peter, probably because he felt more comfortable with me. I nod and ask, "Do you regret your decision?"

Peter sniffs a breath of air. Did my question offend him? He nods before answering.

"Well," he says slowly, "it was pretty bad when my mom got home. Hell, I missed Tiffany and Ally, and I had to do everything for my mom. I slept maybe two hours a night. My mom had to pee all the time, so I would use the sliding board, this thing that looked like a surf board to move her from the bed to the wheelchair and back to the bed. I said, 'Mom, you got to get yourself a new bladder!' It made her laugh. Made me feel a little bit better too. I got Ally every other weekend, so I had two baby monitors, one in Ally's room and one in my Mom's." He lowers his head. "Damn, I didn't know if I was coming or going. Made my mom a peanut butter and jelly sandwich and put it in a brown bag with an apple every morning before I left for work. Then all those doctor appointments. I used the sliding board to get her into and out of the car. She had several appointments every week. I hated those damn waiting rooms. But I was lucky; they were good to me at work and let me take all the time off I needed to in order to help her." He shakes his head contemplatively. "You know, the better my mom got, the worse I became. I drank more and missed Tiffany. Eventually, my mom was able to take care of herself, months later, although it seemed like years. I remember the first time she went back to work. She was all excited and everything. It took a long time for her to drive again. Hell, she didn't even want to get a handicap sticker." He swallows hard. "Yeah, I was a mess by then. So I found Tiffany and persuaded her to marry me. Then we had Clay." Silence for a few seconds. "Eventually we got divorced." He looks up from his downward gaze. "That's okay; guess I had to go through it one more time to know that we weren't for each other."

His eyes narrow pensively, reflectively. Cathartically, Peter has relived a great deal, an emotional cleansing of dirty memories, painful and pernicious; and he has done so with honesty and grit—a quality either taught or inherited from his mother. He looks up, docile smile renewed.

"You know, life is really not that hard. A matter of fact, it's easy. Just don't take anything for granted."

CHAPTER THIRTEEN

Dr. John Cassidy—Physician, Medical Administrator, Humanist

PHONE INTERVIEWS ARE DIFFICULT. Without the personal interaction, facial expressions, mannerisms, gesticulations, and eye contact, much is lost; but Mondays in my office require more energy than other weekdays, and after thirty plus patients, driving to the Texas Medical Center would add insult to injury. And besides, Dr. Cassidy's name was never mentioned by Joyce, Peter, or Lila, only by someone at Beacon. What could he offer? A doctor who is more administrator than physician? "Low expectations" was the catch phrase; but, just like Joyce, you never really know what opportunities may surface from the mundane. Suddenly, her wisdom, learned and experienced, was my new mantra: there is greatness in everything.

"Hello, Dr. Cassidy here."

His voice was soft and gracious, but especially welcoming. After a few pleasantries, his insight about Joyce and his tenacious belief in providing a unique kind of medical care for long-term, debilitated patients, whether stroke or accident, physical or mental, poor or rich, was obvious; metaphorically, a breath of fresh air within a profession clouded with the smog of economics, government inefficiencies, and the insidious poison of medical malpractice.

"Sure, I remember Joyce," he says as if she was an old friend. "Is she all right?" His voice seemed sincere.

"Not only is Joyce all right," I said cheerfully, "she's darn near great, physically and emotionally."

"Yes, she was with us for a long time. Wonderful woman. Everyone loved her—the doctors, staff, nurses, everyone." He pauses, followed by a reflective deep breath. "She was very complicated. Major trauma with the usual mental anguish. "You know, these patients with their poly-traumatic injuries need more than just rehabilitation. They, and their affected family and friends, require more than wound debridement, physical therapy, and medical support. They need psychiatric support as well. This is their new home for months, maybe years, perhaps the rest of their lives, and we must be their extended family. We tried to give this to Joyce."

What—a humanistic physician administrator? His voice rings with genuineness, if only it could be confirmed by looking into his eyes, the window to the soul, then maybe it would be believable.

"I established Beacon back in the early nineties. I didn't want any corporate bean-counter breathing down my neck. These trauma patients needed time and not time limits. I had to fight with Joyce's insurance company a few times, but we got her to stay until we knew she was ready to go home. That's the way it should be."

The phone feels lighter. He is the real McCoy—honest, affable, and most importantly, concerned about the whole patient.

"There was no way I could conform to typical hospital protocols and restrictions. I decided to establish a long-term facility for excellent extended care, as well as an institution that nurtured a patient's physical and cognitive recovery. Not just remedial and out-the-door and good-luck kind of treatment, but a way to help the patient learn how to compensate for their acquired physical limitations and residual pain, for them and their families."

His comments are unimpeachable, his tenets admirable. The medical profession, for all its great technology and research, needs its own shot in the arm, a medical tune-up, perhaps even a pro-verbial resuscitation from the diseases of avarice, commercialism, and conventionalism.

"Once Joyce recovered from her post-traumatic anesthetic amnesia, it took her a few days to comprehend the gravity of her injuries and to accept the long, tedious road to either full recov-ery, or more realistically, partial recovery." He laughs. "Her mara-thoner mentality kicked in. Once she understood her challenges, nothing was going to stop her."

Joyce in a nutshell: strong willed, determined, unflappable.

"I had to talk to her once. I said 'Joyce, dear, now you can't be reading five newspapers while cell phone conference calling and emailing people on your laptop when you can't even get out of bed.'"

He sighs—visions of his unknown face and head, calm and contemplative, probably shaking in disbelief.

"A remarkable woman," he says as an aside. "It is so gratifying to know that one of our family members learned to reintegrate their lives after such trauma." Silence. "I'm so pleased."

With the phone nestled between chin and shoulder, I pound my laptop keys quickly to record his profound words. Later, his background is discovered on the Nexus website. Before moving to Houston, Dr. Cassidy was Assistant Professor at Harvard Medi-cal School and co-founder of the Neuropsychiatry Program at McLean Hospital. Board certified in Psychiatry and Neurology, he has devoted his medical career to treating patients with acquired brain injuries and their associated disabilities. After relocating to Texas, he founded and served as the Chief Medical Officer for the Neurobehavioral Institute of Houston. His bio completes the picture:

> Dr. Cassidy has spoken internationally and authored a number of papers and books dedicated to improving the understanding and treatment of individuals with acquired brain injury. Dr. Cassidy leads the Senior Management Team and is focused on the compa-ny's commitment to quality medical care and its ongoing mission to provide a continuum of care to historically underserved patients and their families in need of specialized healthcare services.

"My Harvard colleagues couldn't understand why I would leave Boston, as if life didn't exist west of the Charles River."

Having trained in Boston, it was easy for me to understand what he said; while vast research programs and a wealth of clinical experience make it one of the finest and most eminent medical communities in the world, a pervasive parochial attitude is tenaciously shared by many in the field. Now with an understanding of Dr. Cassidy the man, his transition to opportunities in another prominent medical community, Houston, is apparent. No vainglorious restrictions for him, just the best for his patients.

"I wasn't going to subsidize our archaic medical care, you know, being told how many patients to see per hour, how many surgical cases needed to be done to make a profit; no, not with these special patients who have been transformed from normalcy to physical and mental disruption, but with a will to live and a desire to compensate for their new handicaps. These patients need exceptional care and at individual paces. That's the only way."

"Dr. Cassidy," I asked, "how did Joyce propitiously end up at Beacon, in the sylvan and bucolic setting of The Woodlands, Texas?"

"Ralph Lilly is a good friend of mine. He took care of Joyce after they knew she was going to survive. Once the surgeons aren't needed anymore, Ralph steps in, like mopping up after the spill, so to speak. Ralph is most happy and vital when he's doctoring. I know he convinced someone in Joyce's family to take her here."

Peter, wanting wise, parental advice, listened to Dr. Lilly's fatherly recommendations, and made a decision, against others' persuading counsel that his mother would be better off at the Texas Medical Center's famed TIRR, or The Institute for Rehabilitation and Research.

"As great a place as it is, I'm not sure Joyce would have done as well there."

I make a mental notation: Must meet this Dr. Lilly, a man who shares Dr. Cassidy's philosophy: a conviction in rehabilitating the physical as well as the mental repercussions of massive body trauma with exceptional medical care and nourishing love.

"Say hello to Joyce for me, please. I'm so proud of her."

CHAPTER FOURTEEN

Remembering Beacon— Joyce's Words

AFTER I "AWAKENED" at Beacon Rehabilitation Center in The Woodlands, I rationalized that if I was going to be leaving in two to three weeks, I had a lot of work to do. I was truly amazed that I could not use the rest room or get up to be in the wheelchair. I could only lie on my back because of the halo and fixator. My right leg had a Velcro cast on it, as did both arms. I had an IV in my right arm and it took some time to realize that I could not move that arm or hand and that it had nothing to do with the IV.

I was on a special bed that had a pump that changed the mattress pressure so that it was more comfortable for me. So far I could only lie in bed. The nurses would adjust the bed so that I began to "sit up," but I could only do it for a short time. I also did "in bed exercises" for my arms and legs. Doing these exercises was painful with the fixator on my leg, but I wanted to do them. I never believed that I would not be able to walk and return to work. It was a matter of how quickly I could do it.

The staff at Beacon was very encouraging. They kept saying I would be running again when I left. I never believed that. I felt that it would only hurt me if I thought of doing so, but I knew I would walk.

After a week or so, the staff came to put me on a "slab" to take me to the whirlpool. It was very painful and took a great deal of time to move me. They said that it was important for skin exfoliation, circulation, as well as my skin grafts on my right thigh.

I took Vicodin before they moved me. As the treatment for the skin graft proceeded, it became more and more painful because they basically debrided it every other day. I asked for additional pain medication before they did the treatment. In one of the final times that I was in the whirlpool, the staff decided that the best approach would be to soak me in the whirlpool and then, when the scab was softened, to rip it off. That was one of my most painful remembrances of my time at Beacon. I learned later that my occupational therapist and the nurses had prearranged this procedure. I was disappointed and hurt by the occupational therapist's participation because she was absolutely wonderful in all of my other treatments and I trusted her.

To this point I had had a catheter and otherwise used a bed pan. After having the catheter replaced a second time, it was decided that I would not have one any longer. I tried really hard not to have to use the bed pan, because it was so hurtful to move.

Three times daily I had injections into my stomach because I was so sedentary and they were concerned about circulation. Also, three times daily, they debrided my stomach incision. I began to anticipate these procedures. They began to represent pain to me. Any movement meant pain to me. Touch meant pain.

My first "doctor's appointment" while at Beacon was to see Dr. Tucker who did a wonderful job of putting my right leg back together. I have a rod for my femur bone, plates, screws, etc. to put my knee together, and a fixator and foot strap for my lower leg and ankle. I was taken in a Beacon van to Methodist Diagnostic. They used a lift to move me from my bed to a wheel chair and then placed me in the van. I was so frightened. They gave me Vicodin and Ativan before I left. It was very painful because I was not used to and had never been in a wheelchair. When we arrived at Methodist Diagnostic, the van could not fit in the entrance, so we had to park approximately a block away. The Beacon personnel wheeled me to my doctor's appointment. By the time I arrived, my pain, increased by my anxiety, was difficult to tolerate. Lila met me at the doctor's office. The doctor could not give me any further pain medication.

X-rays were done on my right leg to ensure that everything "was where it was supposed to be." Transferring to the x-ray table was very painful with the fixator. Lila and the doctor's assistant, Sammy, were so wonderful. Sammy gave me a Butterfinger which I absolutely love, and after that when I went to see Dr. Tucker, Sammy always made sure there were Butterfingers for me.

Dr. Tucker did not understand why I was transported by a van in a wheelchair. After that visit, he required that I be taken by ambulance. The unanswered question was whether the fixator would "put my tibia back together" and make it strong enough to walk on. That question remained unanswered.

Many times I thought that I knew I would recover and return to my life. I knew I could do what everyone at Beacon required of me, but I couldn't reconcile that with their schedule. I am self-disciplined and independent. I did not fit their schedule, but I was going to be okay! Because many of the patients and long-term residents at Beacon have severe brain damage, it was a routine schedule for these patients. I had no doubt that I would do the required therapy, I just felt like I should control when it happened. I was an anomaly! And they were very patient with me.

During this time, I had so many visitors—people that I worked with, friends and people that I knew from the communities and school districts, community college districts, etc. I was so happy for their visits. It was so wonderful. My room was always filled with flowers, DVDs, etc. and visitors. I never felt like I had left my "old world." When these people came to see me, it was always so important to me to know what was happening in their lives. I so enjoyed their visits. I always stayed covered up, except I could not hide my halo and missing teeth. I knew they were very concerned for me, and I wanted to convey how important they were to me and that I would be okay. My concern was not for how I looked, but for the people that were and are so important to me. I did not want them to see the "bad parts of me," yet I had no doubt that I would be back and working with them.

CHAPTER FIFTEEN

Dr. Lilly—
Neurological Savior

THE DRIVE TO DOWNTOWN HOUSTON, usually a nerve-wracking event, is complicated by kamikaze motorists, incessant road work, and the need for pinpoint navigation through convoluted roads that connect hospitals, clinics, and health-oriented schools. Added to this labyrinth is the constant tide of people, waves of patients, doctors, nurses, and health personnel who walk the streets, tunnels, and bridges of the Texas Medical Center, the largest medical complex in the world. Worse, when you finally arrive, parking, limited and sparse, is another burden. On this particular day, the ninety-eight degree July heat was intensified by rays of sun from above and the radiant torridity from the furnace-like pavement below. But what a place—a dynamic mixture of medical vitality and verve, of cancer research, innovative heart surgery, biomedical analysis, and esteemed academics, as well as prime direct patient care given by distinguished physicians and dedicated nurses—a medically focused energy, powerful and unparalleled. The familiar streets were now laced with a new urbanity as a light rail system moved unpretentiously through the medical center's vibrant heart, from downtown Houston, past the museum district, and on towards regal Reliant Stadium, where the "eighth wonder of the world," the Astrodome, sits lonely within its shadow. Perhaps Judge Roy Hofheinz's bombastic reference to the first roofed stadium would have been more apropos to the

Texas Medical Center, a place where people, and not baseballs, take priority.

Rushing late from my morning clinic, the freeway is surprisingly light as green lights greet the entrance onto Fannin Street. An unexpected parking lot with available spots favorably impacts the commute. As if on cue, the elevator door opens with the push of the down button, and without delay, a welcomed air-conditioned walkway leads to one of many professional buildings; but is this where Dr. Lilly is located? Luck? Who knows? but the elevator to floors fourteen and above magically opens and ascends quietly and pleasantly to a well-lit hallway with Dr. Lilly's office, amazingly, staring straight in front of me. It has been forty minutes from door to door, a jaunt of over twenty miles, without interruptions or delays, perhaps a new world record, never to be repeated.

Instead of a traditional door, glass walls expose Dr. Lilly's office to the hallway, and even more unusual, an ornate Western saddle sits majestically upon a wooden carpenter's horse within the waiting room. Comforting? Maybe. Different? You bet. Vanessa, Dr. Lilly's office manager, greets me with a friendly smile.

"Nice to meet you. Dr. Lilly is at the hospital, but I'll call and let him know you're here. Have a seat. Would you like anything to drink?"

Vanessa, as well as the Southwestern décor, is pleasant and reassuring; but something doesn't fit. Prior to this visit, my research and curiosity revealed a photo of Dr. Lilly in the Harris County Medical Society pictorial, a listing of over ten thousand physicians and medical students that compose the largest physician organization in the United States. White hair and beard, Dr. Lilly looks diminutive in the photograph, an uncomfortable suit rising high onto his neck. Where is he from? His credentials reveal graduation from Dalhousie University in Halifax, Nova Scotia. Yet, *Horse and Rider Magazine, Cowboy Gear*, and *Texas Magazine* defiantly sit on a table with Native American paintings and a magnificent earth-tone quilt gracing the subdued yellow walls. The blend is Santa Fe and Wild West—what's an old maritime Canadian doing with this motif?

Standing and stretching helps me unwind the tightened lumbar sacral muscles, tense from the anxious drive to the medical center. Near the entrance to his office is a poster, incongruous with the Western décor: "Functional Areas of the Brain" illustrates the lobes and their associated functions. *Frontal lobe*: behavior, intelligence, eye movement, speech attention, executive function, memory, insight, perception, judgment; *parietal lobe*: voluntary motor movements, sensory perception, pain perception, language comprehension; *temporal lobe:* hearing, auditory memory, visual memory, impulse control, fight-or flight reaction, influences autonomic, nervous system, endocrine function; *occipital lobe:* vision. The brain is a wondrous organ, its convolutions representative of its intricate and complex design and purpose, a system of matter, nerves, and bio-chemicals controlling a body's functions and its emotions, a network so grand in scale that no computer, no matter how sophisticated and advanced, can match.

In front of Vanessa's desk is another glass window with words beautifully etched in Copperplate Gothic style: *Behavioral Neurology: Neurology of Acquired Brain Diseases.* "Acquired" is the magical word—neither genetic nor anatomically incorrect—a misbehaving brain secondary to something that happened or developed, not chosen or given: presumably, a brain that was once normal but now on the fritz; axons and impulses gone wild, out of control, adolescent-like, instead of the soothing purring sound like a well-tuned European sports car. Why is the brain so vulnerable to trauma? Shouldn't the skull be made of something stronger than just a calcified infrastructure of osteoblasts and blood, something like armor, or at least the body of a Hummer? No, Joyce could have been wearing a bank safe, but nothing is invincible when struck by a speeding car.

Another observation: copies of *Highlight Magazine,* that enduring waiting room journal, full of puzzles and stories to entertain the young patient. Maybe a pediatrician, family doctor, or dentist office, but not in *Behavioral Neurology: Neurology of Acquired Brain Diseases.* Funny, the thought of children with brain trauma hadn't registered with me yet, but it makes sense although sad—small brains with injuries: auto, bicycle, swimming, sports, and worse of all, physical abuse. But brain trauma is not selective, so laws about car seats, helmets, no diving zones, and protective gear are necessary. But adult abuse? No, no excuse and unfortunately, no prophylaxis. Suddenly, Dr. Lilly's subspecialty takes on a new meaning, a most difficult field filled with occasional successes but usually tragic in scope.

The door opens and my preconceived image of Dr. Lilly is destroyed. Unlike his photo, Dr. Lilly is tall, rangy, and robust, a neatly pressed white coat covering a black golf shirt and khaki pants. His wide smile is simultaneous with his outstretched hand-shake, firm, confident, and deliberate.

"Hi, come on in. Sorry I was a bit late."

The accent is familiar, neither Texan nor Canadian.

"Have a seat," he says, pointing to a chair next to a large oak table, clean and shiny, scattered books and papers throughout the tabletop. It's a large office, surprising for the medical center where space is at a premium. His office desk is small and set in the corner of the room, but distinctively traditional, contrasting with the Western décor. Shelves of books, all neurological, lace the walls. To the right is a large glass-framed hockey shirt, signed by its previous owner, Bobby Orr. That's it. That's the accent. He's a Bostonian.

"Like the Orr jersey," he says smiling. "Got it at an auction in Dallas." He reflectively rubs his chin, staring at his prize collection. "Do you like hockey?"

Hockey? You mean the sport associated with the jaded joke: two teams were fighting on the ice and a hockey game broke out? Yeah, a fast, daring sport and the darling of Boston where every kid gets skates early and dreams of playing for the "Broons."

Quickly, he turns and grabs something. "Look at this," he orders.

It's a hockey puck in a glass mount inscribed with the words "Dallas Stars, NHL Champions, 1998-99." Impressive, but who is this famous neurologist, Dr. Ralph Lilly?—a man who mops up after the surgeons bring poly-trauma victims back to life, bodies with little life left, near bloodless, with mangled bones and muscles, messed up physiology, and distorted brain function; a doctor who must look at the whole patient, the physical, medical, and emotional repercussions, and most importantly, the survivor's family and friends.

"John Cassidy asked me to move to Houston. He's quite a guy, set up the Neurobehavioral Institute of Houston ... I was at Brown, but I used to practice in Arizona, so I missed the Southwest."

Ah, now the saddle, the décor, and magazines make sense.

"Is she still alive?" he asks.

Who, Joyce? Still alive? What kind of question is that? Joyce is more than alive, she's hearty and vibrant, a strong-willed woman determined to live life to its fullest.

He smiles, a broad, sincere one, a physician who rarely hears of successes like Joyce, a doctor who accepts the harsh handicaps of his patients.

"Good," he says quietly. "That's real good." He leans back in his chair, his face suddenly appearing reflective.

"You know, I never expected to be her doctor."

I'm confused. "Never expected to be her doctor?" I repeat as a question.

He smiles and nods. "Well, it's like this. I remember entering the Surgical Trauma ICU to see a patient, and there is Red Duke at this patient's bedside." He pauses and leans forward. "I'll never forget what I saw. Red had this person cut open, right there on the bed," he says, eyes wide. "I don't think he even had the curtains drawn." He swallows. "I think I saw her intestines laying open." He shakes his head. "Yeah, I'm sure it was. Well, I just turned around and walked away. I thought, no way in hell am I ever going to see that person, he or she'll never make it."

Silence. Even the laptop keyboard is soundless.

"But," he continues, "they consulted me to see this Joyce Lance. I couldn't believe it was the same person Red opened up in the unit. Amazing."

After a hard gulp, my fingers begin to work again typing Dr. Lilly's incredibly haunting observation.

"You know, when I checked her neurological status, nothing was working."

Wow, a body compared to a machine—out of order and under repair.

Dr. Lilly squints. "But I knew something was still there." He sighs deeply and continues. "One of her eyes, darn I don't remember which one, well one of her eyes kept looking around the unit." He shakes his head. "I knew there was something salvageable in her, but I didn't know how much of her nervous system and brain was left."

Just an eye, searching for answers while its master, the brain, slept. No spontaneous breathing, no movement, no reflexes, just one lonely eye, like a lost child, afraid and desperately seeking. No wonder he asked if she was still alive. Although Dr. Lilly was part of her long and anguished-filled recovery and rehab at Beacon, he knew the slim possibilities of full recovery, let alone survival.

"How's Peter?"

The question is unexpected. Sure, what about Peter? But the fact he remembered him and his name is remarkable as well as reassuring. Joyce and Peter were more than a victim/family, the person in bed nine, the auto-marathon runner accident; they were people, unique and distinctive, with names as part of their identity.

"Peter's okay," I tell him, "but still working on issues." Dr. Lilly nods with an understanding, reassuring gesture.

"Poor guy, you could see it in his eyes. He was lost, didn't have a clue what to do. Young and innocent with everyone telling him what to do. He needed help, so I tried."

Lost and seeking, just like his mom's wandering eye, perhaps looking for her son rather than for her own salvation, a natural maternal sacrifice.

Suddenly, Dr. Lilly is more animated. "People just don't get it. Someone gets sick, real sick, and then there's conflict among family and friends about what to do, who to see, what's the best treatment, what doctor or doctors to see, what hospital to go to, etc." His eyes widen. "It's a mess. But just think what it's like when it's a matter of life and death! You understand?"

Yes. Every day, I tend to patients with problems, big problems, who need surgery or are told that they have cancer. Suddenly, family and friends become experts with advice or, sadly, retreat in fear and confusion. Peter was only twenty-one; his mother, his best friend, was near death.

"Damn, they were asking him how aggressive to be with her, like whether to resuscitate her again and about organ donation. Can you imagine how difficult that was for him?"

So Peter tried to drown his fears in alcohol, a means to get through the anguish. But, something visceral and real spoke to him, an inner voice transcending inexperience, naivety, and apprehension, and the strong possibility that he would lose his mother, his family and the foundation of his life. And slowly, he grasped the gravity, holding it tentatively at first, then with a tighter grip, stronger and with resolve, a reaction formed by genetics and nurture. He was his mother's only family member present. He needed to make decisions, hard ones, that he could live with forever; but he needed advice, free from bias and emotion, someone like Dr. Lilly who did more than bring a patient back to life, a doctor who brought patients back to living.

"You need resources, like financial and legal. People just don't get it. Insurance companies are not going to come by your house and hand you a wad of cash. There are serious constraints and bureaucratic BS. Peter didn't know which way to turn. So I helped him. He made the decisions, but I gave him advice when he asked, sound advice, not emotional advice, things that made the decision-making clearer. God knows he needed it."

Dr. Lilly looks at his watch. Lunch is going fast. Neither one of us has much time left.

"When we knew his mom was going to make it, he had to decide where to take her. I know everyone told him about TIRR, but I suggested Beacon."

The Texas Institute for Rehabilitation and Recovery was across The Texas Medical Center campus, famed for its programs and success with trauma patients. Why not there?

"Joyce needed more than just physical rehab. Hell, she needed mental support as well. Brain injured patients are difficult. That's why I suggested Beacon. Yeah, it was far away from Houston, but it was right for her. John Cassidy knew what he was doing when he established it—a center for complete rehab ... speech, occupational, as well as physical. And psych too. The team, me, the shrink, and the rehab folks, met once a week and discussed her progress as well as her needs." He nods. "Peter made the right decision for his mom."

A father figure, mentor, and ally—they all apply to Dr. Lilly. While Peter's dad came through, it was temporary, a man separated from daily decisions by distance as well as by law. Peter was it, and life as he knew it before had changed. His mother was incapacitated, possibly gone completely; the buck stopped with him.

"Tell Joyce and Peter I say hello." He stands tall, grin wide and friendly. Somehow, when he sees his afternoon patients, both adults and children, those with limited memories, slow reactions, visual disruptions, and speech defects within distorted bodies, some ambulating while others wheelchair bound, products of acquired brain injuries, he will think of Joyce and, hopefully, the burden of his work will become a little lighter.

Chapter Sixteen

Medical Records—
Memorial Hermann Hospital

AFTER WEEKS AND SEVERAL ATTEMPTS to obtain Joyce's medical records from Hermann Hospital, the time has come to review the volumes of papers. Before closing the study door, Gizmo, my thirteen-year-old part Shih Tzu and part Lhasa Apso walks in and sits by the comfortable recliner, eyes staring at his master, content just to be in the same room. If Rex, my retired racing Greyhound were still alive, he'd follow the little one in as well, a Mutt-and-Jeff kind of combo, one tall and skinny with a long narrow nose and the other one little and fluffy with a nubbin for nostrils. Rex wouldn't stare at his master, but would promptly fall asleep, a Greyhound's deserving privilege after years of competing, a kind of rest home where napping is king.

Reviewing medical records is a drag; reams of nurses notes, lab and x-ray tests, progress notes, physician orders, forms and permits, and in Joyce's case, numerous surgical notes. But this has a different feel to it. It's Joyce's hospital chart, not one of an unknown patient, and somehow, it's more difficult for me to read, a kind of gut-wrench about someone who is familiar and special.

DATE OF SURGERY 11/06/2000

PREOPERATIVE DIAGNOSIS: Prolonged ventilator support with polytrauma after auto-pedestrian accident including closed head injury, pulmonary contusion, multiple rib fractures, open right tibia fracture, and multiple facial fractures.

POSTOPERATIVE DIAGNOSIS: Same
PROCEDURE PERFORMED: Open tracheostomy
ANESTHESIA: General

DATE OF SURGERY: 11/10/2000
PREOPERATIVE DIAGNOSIS: Scalp avulsion injury
POSTOPERATIVE DIAGNOSIS: Scalp avulsion injury
PROCEDURE PERFORMED: Irrigation and debridement of scalp avulsion injury and primary closure of scalp injury
FINDINGS: Scalp avulsion injury with large subdural hematoma and necrotic debris.
HISTORY: The patient is a 52-year-old white female who was involved in an auto-pedestrian accident on October 20, 2000. The patient had sustained numerous orthopedic and intestinal injuries. At the initial presentation, the patient was bleeding profusely through an avulsion injury on the scalp. The injury was closed very quickly in order to obtain hemostasis. As the patient continued to progress during her hospital stay, the scalp avulsion injury was reassessed and it was determined that the initial closure of the wound was inadequate for proper closure of the laceration. As a result, the oral and maxillofacial team decided to again operate on the patient's scalp avulsion injury.

DATE OF OPERATION: 11/24/2000
PREOPERATIVE DIAGNOSIS: Auto-pedestrian accident with multiple injuries including severe crush injury to bilateral lower extremities; open grade III-B left tibial plateau fracture; open grade III-B left femoral fracture; massive soft tissue loss/necrosis to the left leg, left lower thigh, and left knee; right knee with exposed fractures.
PROCEDURE PERFORMED: Jet lavage debridement and exploration of massive right lower thigh, knee, and right leg wounds and fractures.
INDICATIONS FOR SURGERY: This fifty-two-year-old female was involved in a motor vehicle accident in which she sustained the above mentioned injuries. She was brought to the operating

room today for irrigation and debridement of the massive extremity wounds to avoid sepsis and in preparation for reconstruction.

DATE OF OPERATION: 2/23/2001

PREOPERATIVE DIAGNOSIS: Status post closed fracture right proximal tibia with prior application of Ilizarov external fixator frame.

POSTOPERATIVE DIAGNOSIS: Same plus irrigation and debridement of wound, right proximal thigh.

ANESTHESIA: General

INDICATIONS FOR SURGERY AND FINDINGS: This is a fifty-two year-old white female who was involved in a motor vehicle accident several months ago resulting in multiple injuries. This included a closed comminuted fracture of the right proximal tibia which was treated by application of an Ilizarov external fixation. She also had a skin graft harvested from her right proximal thigh. For some reason, the harvesting site became infected and crusted over. This area was not allowed to be cleaned at the patient's rehabilitation center and it subsequently has become grossly infected and dirty.

DATE OF SURGERY: 2/26/2001

PREOPERATIVE DIAGNOSIS: Granulating wound to right medial thigh and soft tissue necrosis of the scalp.

POSTOPERATIVE DIAGNOSIS: Same

PROCEDURES PERFORMED:

Jet-lavage debridement and exploration of right medial thigh wound.

Split-thickness skin graft from right thigh to scalp with stent.

ANESTHESIA: General

INDICATIONS FOR SURGERY: This fifty-two year-old female is status post auto-pedestrian accident with massive injuries. She had undergone previously a successful reconstruction of her open wounds. She now presents with granulating wound over the medial surface of her right thigh and an area of scalp necrosis.

DATE OF OPERATION: 5/29/2001

PREOPERATIVE DIAGNOSIS:

Nonunion fracture, right proximal tibia

Retained hardware, right proximal tibia

PROCEDURES PERFORMED:

Removal of cancellous lag screw from right proximal tibia; harvesting of right posterior iliac cancellous bone graft; open reduction and internal fixation of nonunion fracture, right proximal tibia with LISS plate and screws with placement of autogenous iliac bone graft to nonunion site

ANESTHESIA: General

Understanding this is not a problem for me; the medical language is familiar like a native tongue; but it's about Joyce. Would the feelings be the same if the patient was a family member or a close acquaintance? It never seems to end, one procedure after another. How can a body, broken and dependent on medications and IV fluids, sustain continuous surgical trauma and repeated anesthesia? Next is Joyce's second admission to Hermann as a transfer from Beacon.

DATE OF ADMISSION: 2/23/2001

DATE OF DISCHARGE: 3/02/2001

TRANSFER DIAGNOSIS: Multiple bilateral lower extremity fracture, status post hardware removal, right lower extremity, and skin graft to right lower extremity and right scalp.

PROCEDURES: Removal of external fixator with irrigation and debridement of old skin graft donor site on the right lower extremity. Re-irrigation and debridement and split-thickness skin graft to old donor side, right lower extremity and right scalp.

TRANSFER DISPOSITION: The patient is to be transferred back to Beacon Health Care.

MEDICATIONS:

Tylenol 650 mg every four hours as needed for pain

Alprazolam 0.5 mg every eight hours as needed for anxiety

Bisacodyl 10 mg.

Benadryl 25 mg. every eight hours as needed for itching

Vicodin one every four to six hours as needed for pain

Morphine 2 mg. intravenously every four hours

Phenergan 12.5 mg intravenously every six to eight hours as needed for nausea

Ancef 1 gm intravenously every eight hours

Colace 100 mg twice a day

Folic Acid 1 mg. every day

Heparin 5000 units subcutaneously every twelve hours

Metoprolol titrate 25 mg twice a day

Multivitamin one every day

OTHER INSTRUCTIONS: Physical therapy and occupational therapy for strengthening range of motion, bilateral upper and lower extremities. Weight bearing as tolerated, bilateral lower extremities for wheelchair transfers only. Bledsoe brace to right leg when out of bed. Dressing changes to the right lower extremity and the scalp per plastic surgery instructions.

FOLLOW-UP CARE: The patient is to follow up with Dr. Tucker in two to three weeks. The patient is to follow up with Dr. Melissinos as instructed by him or his resident.

TRANSFER DIET: Regular

ALLERGIES: no known allergies

HISTORY OF PRESENT ILLNESS: The patient is a fifty-two-year-old white female, well known to Dr. Tucker, who has had multiple procedures on February 2, 2001, to have an Ilizarov external fixator removed without complications, but she was noted to have an infected donor site on her right thigh from a previous skin graft. This was debrided and the plastic surgery service was consulted for treatment.

HOSPITAL COURSE: The patient was admitted to Six West Jones and taken back to the operating room for re-irrigation and debridement and re-skin grafting of her right lower extremity donor site as well as her right scalp. She tolerated this procedure well and was readmitted to the floor for physical therapy as well as for dressing changes. Once cleared by the plastic surgery service, the patient is to be readmitted to Beacon and follow up with Dr. Tucker and Dr. Melissinos as instructed.

Gizmo continues to stare at me with cloudy cataract eyes, heavy eyelids blinking like curtains as the pull of sleep grows stronger. Enough of this. It's too painful for me to read everything. I skip to the end where a perfunctory note, probably dictated by a medical student or an overworked bleary-eyed intern, is printed.

JOYCE LANCE
DOB: 03/10/1948
ROOM: Surgical Trauma Intensive Care Unit
DATE OF ADMISSION: 10/20/2000
DATE OF DISCHARGE: 11/13/2000

This 52-year-old white female was involved in a motor vehicle/pedestrian, high impact accident on October 20, 2000. The patient sustained significant complicated polytrauma secondary to the injury which included multiple orthopedic injuries involving the right femur, right tibia, fibula, right shoulder dislocation, left posterior lateral fibular, and multiple lacerations to the face and scalp. She was admitted to the Surgical Trauma Intensive Care Unit under Dr. James Duke, Trauma Service. Dr. Ralph Lilly was consulted on October 27, 2000.

From her current neurological point at the time of the consult, the patient had also sustained a C2 burst fracture and was currently in a Philadelphia collar with halo. Also, a C3 spinous process fracture and a T4 body fracture occurred as well. In addition, the patient had an abdominal compartment syndrome with a vacuum pump for healing. Facial and scalp lacerations had also been repaired. A CAT scan revealed a contusion to the frontal region of the brain with edema and fluid. An intracranial bolt was placed. The patient was initially responsive and moving all four extremities, but within twenty-four hours, she subsequently became essentially unresponsive and without spontaneous moving to noxious stimuli. A ventilator was used for respiratory support. Initial neurological exam was limited by the nature of the patient's current trauma. Reflexes were difficult to test secondary to the patient's multiple orthopedic trauma. Autonomic changes were noticed on the monitors to pain only. Her initial Hemoglobin was

3 and eventually stabilized to 10 after numerous blood transfusions. Radiology testing revealed a non-displaced frontal fracture with underlying pneumocephalus and possible bifrontal small contusion. CAT scan of the spine revealed comminuted fractures of C2 and stenosis at C4-5 from spondylosis.

Abdominal laparotomy, excision and debridement of wound, and open reduction, internal fixation of femur were performed on October 22, 2000 and a temporary tracheostomy on November 6, 2000.

Physical therapy and occupational therapy were consulted on October 31, 2000 even while the patient was still on ventilator support. The patient stabilized sufficiently to have her arterial line discontinued on November 1, 2000. On November 8, 2000, morphine IV drip was changed to a morphine patient controlled analgesic pump. Speech consultation was requested for swallowing difficulties. The patient was followed on a daily basis by members of the treatment team and medications were reviewed and discussed and adjusted as per symptoms. All members of the team were in agreement to transfer the patient to Beacon Health Facility on November, 13, 2000.

DISCHARGE DIAGNOSES:
1. Closed skull fracture.
2. Open femur shaft fracture
3. Closed C2 vertebral fracture
4. Closed C3 vertebral fracture
5. Closed dorsal vertebral fracture
6. Closed malar/maxilla fracture
7. Coagulation defect
8. Cerebral edema

FOLLOW UP: Dr. Tucker, spinal and orthopedic, Dr. Kushwaha, neurosurgeon, Dr. Yeh, Dr. Duke, Dr. Suko, and Dr. Lilly. Physical medicine and rehabilitation, physical therapy, occupational therapy, and speech therapy.

Gizmo awakens as piles of papers drop to the floor like a sack of potatoes. He watches me as I stretch and think. How did she do it? Survive all this at Hermann and deal with the physically and mentally difficult rehabilitation at Beacon, only to face new obstacles at home? Too much for one evening. Human and dog leave the study, both man and beast need a long walk in the quiet dark evening.

CHAPTER SEVENTEEN

John Klein—Bank Chairman of the Board

"I TELL YOU, it must have been a hell of a transition. I mean, I'm no medical doctor, but to have that kind of injury, all that rehab, and then try to come back to work ... whew!"

John Klein, formerly Chairman of the Board for Klein Bank, an independent local Houston institution before its merger with Southwest Bank, is at his ranch. Joyce worked for him and Michael Brummerhop as their branch administrator.

"Gosh," he says, accent thickly Texan, "she was some worker. She did the marketing, sales, and coordination for our branch expansion." He pauses. "You know, she was the most effective worker I ever had. She had a way of dealing with people unlike most others, kind of like a teacher, a mentor. Heck, she was a teacher in the past, so she knew how to communicate. Everybody liked her."

Klein Bank and Southwest Bank merged in 2004 to become Amegy Bank, the second-largest independent bank in Texas and the fourth-largest bank in the Houston area, behind J.P. Morgan Chase, Bank of America and Wells Fargo. The combined companies had $6.6 billion in total assets, $4.2 billion in loans, $5.3 billion in deposits and a loan limit of $77 million.

"I was at the ranch and didn't learn about Joyce's accident until the next day. And we didn't fully understand the extent of her injuries until we came back to Houston on Sunday. It was so touch-and-go for a while, you know, we didn't really know if she would survive. But she was a runner and was real healthy. But even after we realized she was going to live, I thought she might lose her smarts and way of thinking. Heck, with the grace of God, good medical care, and her dedication and focus, she came back and was the same old Joyce—hard working, determined, and pleasant."

During her recovery, John Klein didn't replace Joyce since other employees pitched in and took over her duties by committee. Why?

He laughs. "Well, I'll tell you. Everyone at the bank, once they knew she was going to survive the accident, had no doubt that Joyce was going to be back at work eventually. They didn't want anyone else but Joyce, so they did her work without any complaints. Amazing. They kept saying that Joyce would be back. Yep, Joyce'd be back. And they meant it too. Really. That's what kind of special effect she had on her co-workers. Real special."

A picture of me in July, 2008 at work at Amegy Bank— what a great bank with great people!

CHAPTER EIGHTEEN

Joyce's Mission

MY PURPOSE IS TO COMMUNICATE to a greater audience that "stuff happens," and that we have it within us to go forward with our lives. Since my accident in 2000, I have talked to individuals about the challenges that they or their loved ones' face. A manager that works for me asked to have lunch. Her husband had been told that he had bile duct cancer and that a liver transplant was not an option. His chances of survival were less than one percent. As we talked, I asked her, the wife, if she remembered what the doctors had said about my chances of survival. She recalled they were very small and that in the next seventy-two hours we would know. I survived, am working, and have a wonderful life. I offered to have her and her husband fly to Mayo Clinic in Minnesota to get a second opinion and stay with my family. She and her husband researched it further and met a doctor here in Houston. The husband had the transplant, is still alive, and working and healthy after approximately three years.

On an individual basis, I have used my experience to help others, whether it be medical, psychological, financial, or concerns about spouses, family and children. Because not many people are marathon runners who get hit by a car going fifty miles an hour, my accident is an extreme example of what can happen. I believe I can help others deal with unwanted events in their lives.

I am willing in any way to help other people help themselves. Maybe it's not just the physical, but rather something that happens to a loved one, a financial dilemma, a divorce, problems with children, etc. I truly believe that we all have it within ourselves to draw from this inner strength to overcome and conquer the unexpected. I remain steadfast in my commitment to help others based on my accident and the amazing and wonderful support I have received and continue to receive. I can give back to people who I encounter on an individual basis.

As I think of all of the wonderful people I am surrounded by, I cannot have, or do not have, any thoughts, feelings, or emotions other than positive ones. I have wonderful friends, my son, grandchildren, Don, my family, and so many others I work with and partnership with in community activities. Because none of us can be in every part of our communities and the various community organizations, I have focused on working with educational foundations and five school districts to support education and preparing students for the real world after school. I get much happiness from these relationships.

I will not say that every moment of my life since the accident has been a "high." Last evening, Don was making dinner and I bent down to pick something up and landed on the floor—my greatest dilemma—how do I get up? Tears came to my eyes, but I wanted to figure out how to get up by myself. I pushed the hassock against the chair and against the wall for leverage and tried to push up with my arms. I cried because I couldn't get leverage with my feet. Don came in the TV room and gently asked how he could help. He placed his feet to help with the traction I needed and then, I was able to get up to the hassock. I cried and cried because I felt helpless. My biggest fear is falling—I can only fall like a tree and then figure out how to get up. Don has a wonderful way of helping while not "helping." Peter and many of my friends and co-workers are the same.

Ally, my granddaughter is amazingly intuitive at the age of five. She reminds her brother that "grama" is "slow" and to wait for me when we are at the park, etc. When she was less than a year old and Peter would take me to my appointments in the medical center, Ally would sit on my lap while Peter pushed the wheelchair. She was like a doll and never moved or cried. It was like she understood.

*My son Peter has three children. Life with grandchildren
can't get any better. Left to right are: Allyson, Addisen and Clay.
Allyson and Clay love having a baby sister, and Grama knows
that she has the most wonderful grandchildren in the world.
Allyson was two months old at the time of my accident and always
was with her father, Peter, as he took me for doctor's visits, etc.
My grandchildren have never known me in my pre-accident life. They
just remind each other that I am slow and they have to wait for me.*

I remember being at Beacon and I would suddenly cry for
no reason. Not frequently, but sometimes. Everyone would be
concerned that I was hurting and I told them that I did not know
why I was crying, that maybe it was just a release. I was used to
running six days a week and my endorphins were in high speed.
I felt my crying was a replacement.

Although I have my "tender moments," I continue to know
that life is wonderful and I enjoy it. I have always believed that I
would continue to get better. I am now facing the possibility that

maybe this is as good as I will get, but I am not ready to accept that yet.

Last evening I went to my massage therapist whom I have gone to since I left the rehabilitation center. She told me of a young man who was in a motorcycle accident last week. He is still in a coma and has a halo, fixator, and other injuries similar to mine. She asked me what she and her boyfriend could do to help this individual. They and their friends were feeling confused on how best to support this man and his family. I suggested that they all donate blood if they could, and that they ask the family and the doctor if there would be value in them talking to the victim even though he was unconscious. They began to do so. Recently, he has begun to react to noises, and now opens his eyes. He still does not seem to "see" people.

My massage therapist asked me lots of questions last evening about my accident because she wants to be able to help the family and friends by understanding my experience. I told her that all injuries are not the same, but I would definitely answer any questions that I could about myself. This group of people has not had a traumatic event like this in their family or circle of friends. She said that by telling them about me, it gives them more hope knowing that someone else had a similar experience and lived. I again reminded her that I am different than her friend, but anything that I could share, I would. She asked me to meet her boyfriend and talk to him so that he could help himself as well as his friend.

The message is simple. We all have it in us to deal with our tragedies/traumas, even if we don't believe that now. We all have it within us—we just need to use it when bad stuff happens.

Chapter Nineteen

Owatonna, Minnesota— Joyce's Hometown

THE CLEAN MINNEAPOLIS SKYLINE, surrounded by a blue cloudless sky, basking in unseasonably high eighty-degree weather, seems incongruous with my mental picture of a cold, overcast wintry downtown where Mary Tyler Moore threw her beret triumphantly upward, a single woman emancipated from the conventional social constraints of her mother's generation. That scene, bombastically rated by *Entertainment Weekly* as the second greatest moment in television history, bears little resemblance to a summerized Minneapolis, pedestrians wearing shorts and tropical shirts happily strolling down Nicolette Street, erasing memories of the endless bitter freezing winds, wet, heavy snows, and depressing early dusks. In the opening scene of that sitcom, Mary Tyler Moore's toothy smile contrasts with a scarf-laden woman who looks disgustingly at the irreverent young lady. This is Minnesota in the dead of winter, her face states disapprovingly; you're not supposed to be happy, but stoically tough, hardened by the deadened gray overcasts and lifeless bare tree limbs. As the vehicle turns right onto Interstate 35 South, Garrison Keillor's roguish comment that the Minnesota "women are strong, the men good looking, and the children above average," rings with witty verisimilitude, a Midwestern mantra created by harsh environment, fundamental Lutheran doctrines, and Nordic cultural resolve. It was on *Prairie Home Companion,* that radio bastion of creatively corny vaudeville shticks, that Keillor comically asks, "How many

Minnesota Lutherans does it take to change a light bulb?"—"five," he answers in his classic deadpan style, "one to change it and the four others to prepare the potluck dinner."

The road winds lazily through undulating countryside, green blankets of cornfields, grain elevators, and, surprisingly, retail centers, statements as irreverent as Mary Tyler Moore's midwinter jubilance. I'm in Minneapolis for a nephew's wedding to a native Minnesotan, and take the opportunity to drive my rented car to where Joyce was born and raised, Owatonna, about sixty-five miles south of the big city. Another phrase comes to mind, this time coupled with Richard Rogers' sweet music: "the corn is as high as an elephant's eye"—only this is Minnesota, soul of the heart land, and not the dusty, tornado-prone land of Oklahoma. Meeting Joyce's family, at least part of her family, is an honor; but discussing her accident and recovery may be a challenge. Her sister-in-law's cheery phone voice is encouraging, but what about her brother, the eldest of the five siblings, and especially Joyce's father, widowed just two years ago? The unadorned green interstate sign indicates Owatonna, next two exits, a farming town with a population of twenty thousand. The city's website boasts "the heart and heartbeat of a greater community known as Southern Minnesota," followed by the phrase, "where progress and history entwine."

After driving in the wrong direction, I call Alice, Joyce's sister-in-law, who navigates me to *The Kernel Restaurant* just past the old *Sinclair* station. Preconceived images are destroyed and the iconic picture of the man and woman in Grant Wood's American Gothic fade quickly. The famous painting from 1930 depicts the essence of Midwestern themes, but was the artist glorifying rural American morality, or satirizing a hidden myopic repressive regionalism that Wood, a native Iowan, witnessed and understood? No, Joyce's brother, Ken, without overalls, doesn't look like he just came off the farm. His handshake is firm and genuine; but it's Elmore, Joyce's and Ken's father who appears slightly enigmatic, an old baseball cap, worn and weathered, covering his bald pate and shadowing a soft, sun-blemished face. His weaker handshake indicates either a healthy suspicion about the big city doctor's visit or elderly poor health. Both guesses are wrong and right at the same time.

"We thought you might like coming to this restaurant," Alice chirps, "you know, more like home-cooked food."

"Yep," Elmore adds with a subtle wink. "Anybody can go to Appleby's."

His warm, slightly sly smile reveals wit rather than a superfluous platitude. He may be old, but his mind is neither jaded nor flat; a retired farmer who discerns more than rows of corn and soybean. He pulls a folded envelope from his baggy pants pocket and slowly, deliberately, opens it.

"Here," he says softly, "are some photographs of Joyce."

It's Joyce and her siblings, all smiling, with a cloudless blue sky behind them. No one knows the date, but Ken's short-sleeve shirt indicates summer, each person appearing healthy, ruddy, and content. Joyce is easy to pick out, her naturally curly blond hair stylishly befitting her sanguine face. Next to her is Kate, then Sharon, with Jeanette, the youngest, furthest to the right. They're a handsome clan, vibrant and hearty.

"That's Jeanette," Ken says pointing his index finger to the one who died at the age of thirty from Hodgkin's Lymphoma. "She went to Omaha to get treatment, an experimental procedure," he says solemnly. Instead of misty eyes, his stare is surprisingly void of emotion. Why? His obvious gentleness begets a sensitive man—a psychological defensive mechanism hiding a deep, painful sorrow? Elmore shows the next photo.

"That's our house," he reports confidently. But an uncomfortable moment's hesitation suggests a memory problem as the old man rubs his chin. "The dog," he says referring to the white hound in the foreground, "what was his name, Kenny?"

Ken is puzzled as well. "I think Scuffy, Pa. Yeah, Scuffy."

Elmore nods. "Yep, the police dog." His hand shakes slightly as he displays the next one. "Here's Joyce painting her house in South Dakota." The foxy grin returns. "Joyce did everything. Taught German and fixed up the house as well. You know, she always did that, and taught them underprivileged kids too. At Mankato, then Gettysburg, South Dakota, then in some coal min-

ing town in West Virginia, Florida, then Honduras. I liked that
town in South Dakota ... small, but real friendly people there."

Why so many places? No one offers an explanation, but
Elmore's comment about all the things Joyce did intimates an oc-
cult acrimony towards her husband, albeit discreet and without
pejoration.

"Here's one with Joyce and Peter." Triumphantly, mother and
son display their trophy of fish, a mutual love for the sport shared
with gramps as well.

The waitress comes by and takes our orders. Elmore knows
exactly what he wants. He sips his water, takes his hat off, and
pulls the last photo from the envelope.

"This is one of Joyce running a marathon. He scratches his
bald head. "Don't know which one it was or when, but it's a
marathon."

Focused and paused, the moment catches Joyce running in
Memorial Park, Houston, the elevated freight train tracks behind
her, but who took the photo? Ken, Alice, Elmore, a sister?

"Don't know. None of us were there."

The lack of knowledge contrasts with their obvious pride. Was
Joyce a good athlete as a child? All look blank.

"Well," Alice replies, "there were no girls' sports in those days,
so no one really knew."

A different zeitgeist: Joyce, young, hardy, energetic, worked
the farm chores, pitching hay and shoveling hog manure instead
of gymnastics or softball. Critics of the pig industry claim that ten
thousand hogs can produce as much waste as a city of twenty-five
thousand, a tough business, now corporate controlled. Elmore
takes two papers from the envelope.

"I wrote some things down for you," he says calmly. "Things
I could remember about Joyce."

The small, uneven penmanship is difficult to read:

Joyce was baptized at Aurora Lutheran Church. Confirmed there
also; went to county school and Owatonna High which she graduated from; she graduated from Mankato State University; she ran in
a number of marathons; Joyce taught and was a business manager
for the district in Gettysburg, South Dakota; after high school in
Owatonna, Joyce worked in a bank in Mankato; when war in Viet

Nam drafted her husband, David, they moved to Missouri and then to Germany; Joyce worked in the officers' corporation; when his term of army was over, they came back to Mankato for more college; they applied for a job teaching school in Welch, West Virginia, teaching German a couple of years in Copenhagen, Denmark; they went to teach in Honduras; when they moved to Houston, Joyce went to work for Commonwealth Savings and Loan.

Elmore's assorted written memories come from an older mind, a reservoir of years of farming and raising a family, a collection of thoughts, although somewhat disconnected, reflecting highlights of his daughter's past. The waitress brings the lunch plates. Elmore is hungry and digs into his open-faced steak and gravy sandwich with gusto, memory lane on temporary hold. The restaurant is warm, the strong, heated sunlight pouring through the window onto the table, while a pesky fly, apparently annoyed for not being invited, audaciously irritates each patron. Unsure if the timing is right, the silence is broken when I ask them about the moment they learned of Joyce's accident. Focused on his meal, Elmore is too busy to respond and Alice politely defers to Ken. The oldest sibling wipes his mouth with a paper napkin and stares at scrambled eggs and pieces of ham.

"Well, I was at the house when the phone rang," he says dispassionately. "At first, I thought it was some telemarketer, you know, trying to sell me something." He looks up, clear eyes straight ahead. He smiles. "I almost hung up on her." He picks up his fork, and like bailing hay, stuffs a sizeable amount of food into his mouth, chews slowly, and takes a large gulp of water. What is he feeling—the painful moment, the horror of Lila's words? But he continues matter-of-factly. "Then I heard something about the bank I knew Joyce worked at, so I listened." He pauses and slowly rolls his water glass in a circle on the table, like effortlessly ice skating on a carefree winter Minnesota Sunday afternoon, chores done and permission granted to be a kid. "She said that Joyce was in an accident and hurt real bad." Deliberately, he releases his grip on the glass and tightens his lips. "She said it didn't look good."

Alice stops eating and looks at her father-in-law whose healthy appetite continues to take priority over conversation. Ken continues, but this time, his eyes are narrowed and mouth

On the day of my accident, Lila called my parents to tell them
of the accident. My brother, Ken, was with my parents
when Lila related the news of my serious accident.
Left to right: Joyce; my dad, Elmore Sorenson;
my brother, Ken Sorenson, and his wife, Alice Sorenson

slightly contorted. "I asked her if Joyce was dead. Yeah, I said, 'Is she alive or dead?'"

Elmore's eyes, once glued to his meal, wander upward, void of facial expressions, but his ears intently listening to his son's recollection.

"Lila said she was alive for now, but she'd know more later. Then she asked me not to tell my parents. She didn't want them to worry."

All three sit at the table, neither eating nor speaking. Finally, Ken continues.

"Pa was out on the tractor, so I went out and got him. We sat in the living room waiting for Lila to call back." Surprisingly, Ken has nothing else to add and returns to his meal. As if on cue, Elmore takes over.

"We just sat there. Nothing any of us could do."

His response is unexpected. How could a father just sit there and wait for a call about his oldest daughter's life, an emotional detachment beyond comprehension? Suddenly, it becomes apparent.

"You know, it's just like farming," he says. "You work and you expect losses...that's life's ups and downs. Guess we'd always lived that way." He rolls his tongue across his teeth. "I couldn't do anything for Joyce now. It was out of my hands. No point wasting energy on it. She was going to live or die without my worry."

His simple, yet profound, comment comes from a man who's faced the vicissitudes of life head on, like the Jaguar that hit Joyce at fifty miles an hour—a startling revelation, free of judgments or criticism, a tenacious belief in accepting the uncontrollable and fundamentally intrinsic circumstances of living, an acknowledgment of life's tapestries. Elmore takes a deep breath and continues eating, a bead of sweat sits alone beneath his left eye—or is it a tear drop? Suddenly, the table is silent, all eating perfunctorily, thoughts about that day. Now it's apparent; Joyce's family feels deeply, but not demonstratively, emotions raw and real, but contained within, like protection from the bitterly cold winter winds that cross the upper Midwestern plains, Canadian arctic fronts, powerful, chilling, and relentless.

Alice breaks the silence. "We visited Joyce later, after she was home. Peter took care of her, but she was hurtin', bad, real bad."

Is this the time—the moment I ask about his relationship with Peter? From the photos, it's easy to discern; Peter and Gramps were an item, sharing summers and fishing. Why the estrangement?

Just like his son, Elmore moves the water glass in circles, although in a slower, more contemplative way than Ken, and ponders the inquiry.

"Well, I guess Peter didn't like the way I told him to take care of his mother. I was just trying to be helpful, but I guess it bothered him."

Joyce's accident, the loss of his wife, and missing his grandson is analogous to the strains and frailties of farming as well as to the bigger picture, life itself.

Elmore has finished lunch but not his thoughts. "You know, it must have been real hard for the lady who hit Joyce."

Hard for the lady who hit Joyce? Is Elmore joking? After all discussed, he feels sorry for someone he doesn't know, the one who almost killed his oldest daughter. Pensively, he places his arms on the table and leans forward, his back slightly crooked from years of raw physical labor.

"I'm sure she felt bad about what happened," he says sincerely.

He's serious and neither Ken nor Alice disagrees with him. How can a man, whose daughter was hit by a speeding car, fighting for her life, years of surgery and rehabilitation, forever changed physically, not be angry with the driver? He answers himself.

"You know, things happen. You just got to accept it."

Is his attitude an exception to the rule, a product of sustained losses, upbringing, Midwestern values, religious beliefs, or an intrinsic part of his DNA? Can such an outlook be achieved or given, nurture versus nature? Suddenly, Elmore looks sleepy after his hearty meal, or is it the weight of those heavy and unpleasant memories that is enervating? The waitress comes with the check, but Ken outreaches all and grabs it.

"My treat," he commands.

His generosity is appreciated, but it's more than that. He is the oldest, the one responsible for their land, their crops, and their family. Pa is old, widowed and slightly devitalized, and Ken, never one to shirk his responsibilities, needs to assert himself, even if it's paying the bill.

"They have wonderful desserts here," Alice says while pointing to the glass enclosed shelves.

Elmore, suddenly revived, smiles. "Heck, I can get me one of those pies and take her home and eat it later."

His quirkiness elicits laughter, but his realistic reasons make sense. He's no fool. He may be old, but not unwise. Outside *The Kernel*, good-byes and handshakes conclude our restaurant meeting, but Ken offers more.

"Do you want to see Owatonna?" he asks sincerely.

See it? Heck yes. I want to see as well as absorb Joyce's childhood environment. Ken climbs into the front seat of my rented Pontiac Grand Prix and points to the right.

"Let's head into town," he says as if I was a native.

Owatonna is quaint; small, neat houses line the tree-lined streets. Ken shows where he used to "cruise" downtown, past Owatonna High School, the movie theater, and the few stores along Main Street.

"Not much industry here," he adds. "Sure not the same as when we grew up. Heck, there's crime here now, never used to be."

What type of crime?

"Well, robberies, even a murder," he says while staring straight ahead and not elaborating. "Turn here."

The small town scenery is gone and wide fields of corn and soy seem endless.

"I own all these fields, but rent it out to other farmers." His inflection suggests disappointment. "Can't handle all of this, so I got me a real job. I work the night shift at Wal-Mart." He grins and pats his abdomen. "My own kind of aerobics. Heck, if I didn't do that, my stomach would be out to here."

Works the crops during the day and stocks the shelves at night—does he ever rest? He points toward buildings about a quarter of a mile away.

"That's a pig farm over there. Corporate pigs."

Corporate pigs?

"Yeah, you know, big companies own the hogs and pay the people to farm them." He shakes his head slowly. "Not like it used to be."

Ken doesn't amplify his comment, but further research confirms his lamentable statement. The number of hog farms in the United States decreased from over 640,000 in 1969 to less than 150,000 by 1994. In 1995, farms with two thousand or more hogs accounted for forty-three percent of all hog farms. The twelve largest producers owned twenty percent of the nation's sows in 1996. Ken's comments are consistent with increasing public sentiment towards corporate, mega hog farming. Don Webb, founder of the Alliance for a Responsible Swine Industry and Citizens Against Corporate Hog Factories, states, "I have no problems with the hog industry growing hogs, but I want them to be responsible. I don't believe that one American has the right to force the odor of feces and urine down another American's nose. And I don't think they have the right to threaten the water supply." Also, critics contend that manure handling on mega-farms is a disaster waiting to happen as well as the possibility of long-term health problems due to odor from hog operations and reduced real estate property values. Yet, supporters of mega-producers state that contracting allows more families to stay in farming by reducing financial risk.

"Turn left," Ken says laconically.

I recognize it immediately from Joyce's photos—her one-room school house, sitting on a treeless plot of grass, the building appearing old, worn, and lonely. While it is currently used as a municipal facility for the rural town of Havana, Minnesota, there is no marker commemorating its historical significance—a place for elementary education, maybe twenty-five to thirty students, ages from six to thirteen, who called it their school; children of farm families who were expected to contribute by doing chores; impressionable children who didn't recognize swine odors emanating from their clothes and permeating the one room, but who listened to a dedicated teacher who taught them lessons about history, math, and science, a respite from the mundane and hard labor of their home life.

Ken smiles and points across the road. "There's the well where we got our water for school." He shakes his head slowly, memories from long ago revived. "It sure was tough in the winter," he says prosaically, yet profoundly. He takes a deep breath—reflection or acceptance of his childhood thoughts. "Let's see the church," he says without emotion.

In the silence, images of Joyce in that small school, learning lessons well, listening to adventurous topics about Asia, Europe, and Africa; readings about wars, exploration, discoveries, inventions; instruction about numbers, mathematical escapades leading to abstract formulas and solutions; and stories about royalty and paupers, exploits and mysteries. She soaked it all in and took her edification home while tending to the hogs and the corn.

As if on cue like a tour guide, Ken points to a building up the road.

"There's the church we used to go to."

The unassuming Lutheran church blends well into the countryside, a white citadel of faith among the austere, if not brutal, environment. Are Jeanette and your mother buried in the cemetery next to the church?

"Nope, they're buried near the freeway. That's where the family plots are."

I'm surprised when he says this. "Why not at the church?"

Ken sighs. "We don't go here anymore."

The window to the past opens slightly. When and why did Joyce's family leave the church? Was it after Jeannette's death or after Joyce's accident? It's easy to read Ken now; the tone of his voice and his subtle mannerisms suggest a sensitive subject, something that must remain closed and hidden.

"Let's go to the house," he says abruptly. On command, I pull away from the church, and like the vehicle, Ken navigates to another topic, a more comfortable and familiar one—farming.

This is the little church that I attended until I graduated from high school. Aurora Lutheran Church is still a wonderful church with wonderful people attending it.

"We harvest the corn in October," he states didactically. "Big demand for corn now since we're part of the ethanol group." He doesn't elaborate, but the current political push for cheaper fuel favors the corn farmers, a rare advantage for the agricultural industry. Later, after perusing several corn trade websites, one succinct paragraph states it best:

> Corn is in the food on your plate—and perhaps even in the plate itself. Corn is in the fuel tank of your vehicle and possibly in the comforter on your bed. It's in your soft drink. It's in your windshield wiper fluid. For hundreds of years, corn production has been a source of constant strength for America—providing a solid foundation for our nation's sustenance, stability, security and success.

Bold or embellished? Ken wouldn't care. His dedication to farming transcends politics, finance, and agricultural science; he and the land are one.

Suddenly, Joyce's quaint and clean childhood home is in sight, a white house sitting on a well manicured, deep green lawn, hog house tucked behind. Ken gazes at the barn as if he hasn't seen it in years, probably recollecting favorably of a different time when the farm was alive and active, his father on the tractor, mother in the house, and he and his siblings working together, a common cause, a family unity.

"Not much going here now," he laments.

Alice appears; her spontaneous hug feels right.

"Now if you have any further questions, just call or email me," she offers sincerely.

Ken chuckles. "Don't email me," he says defiantly. "I don't know how to use a computer and I don't want to either."

She smiles. "Come back and we can go to Rochester and see the Mayo Clinic. You'd probably like that."

The ride back to Minneapolis looks different now. The long rows of corn and soybean are natural majestic icons of those who work the soil with their sweat and achy muscles, whether the air is thickly humid and warm or bitterly and biting cold; but the ability to surpass the inequities and hardships of farming goes beyond the physical, and Elmore, the patriarch of Joyce's family, said it best with his simplistic yet powerful words. His family looks further beyond what is good and what is bad. Life doesn't always go the way you've hoped or expected, but that doesn't really matter. If one searches hard enough, there is good in the unexpected as well; then there is nothing to be sad or angry about. Peter, for all the difference in his upbringing and genetics, stated the same thing: "You know life is really not that hard. A matter of fact, it's easy. Just don't take anything for granted."

An epiphany appears; Peter and Gramps, while not physically together, are one, a bond strong and irreproachable; and Joyce, the daughter and the mother, with her instinctive wisdom, cherishes it. It's her father's gift to her, now bestowed generously and lovingly to her son, and nothing, not even a Jaguar at fifty miles per hour, can destroy it.

CHAPTER TWENTY

Joyce's Words

I RECEIVED AN E-MAIL FROM ALICE and talked to Dad and they very much enjoyed the time Randy spent with them. Since I was eighteen, I have always been "the daughter/sister on the phone." I am the exception in my family as everyone else lives in Owatonna, Minnesota.

On July 4th, Peter brought the children to the condo so that they could swim. Allyson and Clay have been taking swimming lessons and they love to swim. They were both swimming when Clay declared that he needed to go to the rest room. Ally continued to swim, but she wanted to try some further distances. Don did not have on his swimming attire and I had on one of my running shirts and jersey work-out pants. I started to get in the pool, confident that if anything happened Don was there. Ally called to me, "Grama, you can't get in the pool." I told her I could, as I walked down the steps. Ally said, "But Grama, your legs." Not because of anything I have said, but because she sees that my knees do not bend like most people. And she is only five years old! We had a great time, and when Peter came back with Clay, I saw the astonished/concerned look on his face. I exited the pool.

This experience reminds me of my time at Beacon. At first I could not move at all. Then I began bed exercises. Then they began to elevate my upper body so I could get used to not being flat in bed. I don't know why, but it was exhausting.

When they changed my bed linen, it was an exhaustive undertaking. Bed baths and using the bedpan were tiring because it took energy I did not have and was painful. However, I knew that if I did not "move," my chances of "being alive" were less.

The first time that they took me out of my bed to move me to a transport table to go to the whirlpool was the first time I realized, or it became clear to me, how immobile I was. Being turned in my bed to put the "sling" under me so that they could use the lift and move me to the transport table was painful but also made me suddenly realize what I needed to do to get back to my life. Someone had to hold my halo, another person my fixator, and then the "sling" to move me. And, man, was that transport table hard and flat!

After several trips to the whirlpool, because of my skin graft sites, I did not continue the whirlpools. They became concerned about a possible infection in my donor site for the skin graft. I returned to bed baths and elevated bed time. They also began to sit me up in a wheelchair for several hours at a time to prepare me for being in an upright position.

Monday through Friday while I was at Beacon, I did exercises in my bed for my legs and arms. The therapist would help me move my leg with the fixator. My right arm and hand were still immobilized. My bed was elevated to a semi-sitting position and I was "lifted" to the wheelchair for an hour or two. This was a difficult exercise as they forced my legs to fit in the foot slots. My knees did not bend very well, so this was painful. I was always relieved when I could get back in bed, but also understood that I needed to do this.

While I was at Beacon, I made numerous trips to Hermann Hospital and Methodist Diagnostic Clinic for appointments with my doctors. The first time I went, I was taken in a Beacon van in a wheelchair. They gave me pain medication before I left. After having x-rays, etc., I was very tired and in pain. Lila met me at the doctor's office and spoke to Dr. Tucker who directed Beacon in the future to transport me by ambulance. I never thought of "complaining" about my transportation, but Lila sensed my pain and talked to Dr. Tucker and the people at Beacon. She was there for me when I accepted what was happening to me. I never thought to complain. I thought it was all part of getting better. I lived with pain. I knew that touch, bed baths, physical therapy, and many other routine things meant pain. I dreaded the pain, anticipated the pain, experienced the pain, and was always relieved when I was back in my bed and could just lie still. I knew I needed to do all of these things for the long-term results that I wanted—to return to my normal life. But most immediately, it hurt lots!

My initial days at Beacon were filled with pain and pain medication. At the same time, I was surrounded with all of the wonderful staff at Beacon as well as the many people that came to visit me, whether from the bank, people I knew in the community and school systems, etc. I always knew that I had the most wonderful support any person could ever expect, but I remained impatient to be repaired and back to life.

CHAPTER TWENTY-ONE

Connie Bock—
Joyce's Childhood Friend

ANOTHER DRIVE INTO HOUSTON as the late afternoon daylight shines brightly though the right car window—this time I'm a passenger going to a medical conference. This is a good time to call Connie Bock on my cell phone. She and Joyce met in high school, became close friends, and maintained their relationship sharing the good memories while attentively listening to each other's highs and lows.

"My daughter, Melissa, and I were to meet Joyce that weekend. We came down to Houston once a year. Little did we know that we would be helping Peter while Joyce lay in a coma."

Not seeing her made it difficult to read Connie, but her cheerful voice and optimistic attitude felt right. A lot like Joyce; easy to see why they were friends.

"Oh, it was so tough those first few days. I knew what was going on since I'm an ICU nurse."

Interesting perspective. Here is someone, a loving friend, who understood the medical gravity. Was it harder for her than those who knew little about trauma? Connie pauses before answering.

"No, I knew that Joyce might not survive. But on the other hand, I knew she had a chance for several reasons. First, her strength and health, second, being so close to a level three trauma center, and lastly, because she was injured on a major road instead of some side street that would have taken an ambulance longer to find and get to."

On the day of my accident, my life-long friend, Connie Bock, and her daughter, Melissa, were flying in from Minnesota to vacation with Joyce. When they arrived, they were not aware that I had been in an accident. They stayed in Houston for several weeks to be with me and help Peter. Connie and I attended high school together, and Connie is a friend who everyone wishes to have—dear, sincere, always there, looks at the best in every situation and is lots of fun. Left to right: Connie, Melissa, and their dog, Charlie.

She's right. For the severity of her injuries, Joyce was fortunate that her accident occurred close to The Texas Medical Center.

"You know, with the amount of blood loss she had, just a few minutes longer and she might not have made it, or she might have sustained enough anoxia to create brain damage."

Connie is sharp, just like most ICU nurses, RNs who grasp clinical medicine, a breed apart.

"And the Surgical Trauma ICU, well, I was used to the mess, the blood, the monitors, the alarms, and the chaos. It frightened

Peter and Lila a lot, but I knew better. Maybe it gave me more optimism. You know, this was a first-rate facility, no small town ICU. These nurses and doctors were good." She sighs. "Yes, Joyce was lucky."

Some of my papers fall to the car floor when a speeding truck cuts sharply in front of us. My laptop is at home and the chicken scratch penmanship is especially straggly.

"Lila and I were allowed to see Joyce often. They were so kind there. We would talk to her, touch her, and hold her hand and pray." She pauses again. "I just had this feeling that Joyce knew we were there."

Just like Joyce—hopeful, sanguine, and strongly spiritual. Was she like this as a teenager?

"No," Connie says softly, "not really. I guess I would call Joyce quiet, intelligent, good natured. This strength of hers, this ability to pull herself up when everything was tough, surfaced after her divorce."

More interesting insight.

"You know, Joyce was determined to have a career. First, she taught German in South Dakota, then West Virginia, then Honduras. Peter was born in South Dakota, you know."

Yes, Elmore may have mentioned that, but Connie's reference to work and parenting is consistent with that era. Wonder if Joyce would have done that today, separate career from motherhood.

"Joyce and I spent some time in Europe. We had so much fun."

Europe?

"Yes, she took a position there for a short time teaching English in Copenhagen. I met her there and we toured all of Europe."

"Where was Dave, Joyce's husband?"

Connie pauses. "Oh, he stayed in the States."

Her comment goes no further. Connie is discreet and offers nothing else; perhaps she sensed marital discord even then.

"Joyce worked in a bank in Mankato, so when they transferred to Houston, she went back to banking instead of teaching. I guess she felt there was more opportunity in it."

More opportunity, or was it for survival? She and Dave soon divorced. Your view of Dave?

Connie sighs. "Well, Dave and I got along. We both stayed with Peter after Joyce's accident for a few weeks." She pauses again, perhaps looking for a diplomatic phrase.

"All I can say is that Joyce's parents didn't approve of her marriage."

Okay, enough on that. Connie is classy, astute, and generous; no need to be rude. Change subjects: was Joyce athletic in her youth?

"No, not that I could recall. Remember, there wasn't much opportunity for women sports in those days."

Consistent with Alice's statements, but Connie adds another twist.

"Joyce was focused on staying slim and slender."

"Why?" I asked, sensing a deeper reason other than image.

"Well, her mother fought with her health and weight for many years and I think it bothered Joyce."

Hmm. Mother/daughter conflict? Connie is tactful—her personality or her respect for Joyce's privacy; maybe both. "What about Peter?"

Her voice is cheerful again. "Oh, that Peter, he's such a sweet, sweet boy, so loving to his mother and kids." Another deep sigh. "He had some tough decisions to make, about his mom, the finances, his own life. But he never complained. I used to tell him over and over, 'Peter, there is no one else in this world who loves your mother as much as you. Any decision you make will be the right one."

Profound. It takes effort to scribble her comment while the car turns onto South Post Oak in uptown Houston.

"But you know Peter made the right decision about Beacon. Oh that place was just excellent—everything about it from the doctors, to the nurses, to the therapist. I've never seen a place quite like it; I mean they made Joyce feel like this was her second home."

I know it's difficult to bring up, but I need to ask. "Why was there conflict between Peter and his grandfather?"

"Yes, so sad. Peter was being pressured by friends to send his mom to the rehab center at The Texas Medical Center, but he was convinced Beacon was better, and he was right!"

Suddenly, my cell phone feels heavy, held with a tightened right hand. Is there more?

"Well, I think Lila was so worried about Joyce that she called up Elmore and asked him to talk to Peter. It wasn't anything big, but Peter took it hard. He wanted his grandfather to support him, not criticize him, but I don't think that was Elmore's intentions at all." Another moment of silence. "Those two really love each other. Peter would come up to Minnesota and spend the summer with gramps and Elmore loved having Peter with him. Maybe they'll get back together."

Consistent with all the others—Peter and his grandfather, pals. Why can't they reunite?

Connie pauses. "Well, I hope they do. They should."

She offers no more about the grandfather/grandson estrangement.

"Peter worked so hard when his mom came home from Beacon. He did so much for her." A surprise laugh. "Did Peter tell you about the Fisher-Price walkie-talkies?"

Some vague recollection.

"Yes, he used the intercom for his mom that he used for Ally!"

And why not? A perfectly good system for an adult as well as for a baby.

"Anyway, Peter never complained about what he did for his mother. I mean, he took care of her, drove her to all her many, many doctor appointments, managed the finances, and cleaned the house a little."

Connie's chuckle indicates some ironic jocularity—a twenty-one-year-old man/boy being neat? Maybe.

"I just remembered something. I came down to visit Joyce at Beacon and she begged me to take her out for a ride. The staff said no, but Joyce was so persistent that they agreed to let me drive her around the parking lot once and only once. Well, Joyce had no intentions of shortening her first outing since her accident. So we kept driving around the parking lot. We both waved as we passed the staff outside the front door, all of them giving us dirty looks. Oh my, Joyce and I laughed and laughed. It was really good for us."

Two high school chums cruising the rehabilitation center. Hey, it raised Joyce's spirits, something she needed and deserved.

"You bet it did. And for me as well."

Just like Dr. Lilly said. These accidents affect everyone—family, friends, and workers. It's late and I don't want to keep Connie any longer. "Any further comments?"

"There aren't many women like Joyce, so determined to make the best of what she has. And you know, in spite of her accident, she feels blessed. She adores her grandchildren, loves Don, and enjoys the challenges of her banking career. No, Joyce may have had a little detour, but she's back and better for it."

The early evening air feels comfortable and pleasantly warm, a nice feeling after the frigid auto air-conditioning. My right hand relaxes, but my mind still whirls with thoughts, another testimony to Joyce and her life, her friends, her miraculous recovery. Maybe the medical meeting this evening won't be so bad after all.

Chapter Twenty-Two

Dr. Jeffrey Tucker— Orthopedic Wizard

From Lila's Notes

Meeting Notes
Joyce Lance With Dr. Jeffery Tucker
1/22/01—10:00 A.M.
Dr. Jeffery Tucker- Orthopedic Surgeon
Diagnostic Professional Building

Joyce and transportation were late for meeting as the eight-foot van could not access the Diagnostic Center handicap access with a six-foot garage clearance. Joyce very frustrated, tired, and groggy.

Dr. Tucker was given the PT notes, CAT scan films, list of medications and was told Joyce had received 2 Darvocet tablets and .05 Advanol, per Susan at Beacon.

There were no films of the femur or any films of the legs in the two packages of film provided. Dr. Tucker required x-rays for his review and assessment. This was extremely painful for Joyce to be lifted to the x-ray table and moved to accommodate the x-rays.

Dr. Tucker expressed surprise at the limited range of motion in her legs and asked if she had been receiving any therapy. He noted this was his first meeting with Joyce since she had left Hermann.

Dr. Tucker reviewed x-rays. Directed *no weight on either leg for at least two months.* Ordered range of motion therapy; his orders were given to the transport ladies. He also asked why the lock was still on the cast for her left leg. This restricted her ability to bend the knee. His assistant released the lock at Dr Tucker's request.

Dr. Tucker noted he had not done a knee replacement in her left knee allowing the knee time to heal, if possible. He strongly believes she will need a full knee replacement to heal properly. Will wait two months to make that decision. Predicts the knee will not do well in therapy. Swelling and discoloration in both legs was noted which was likely due to the extensive time she had been sitting in the wheelchair.

The right leg is healing. The metal rod in right femur is permanent and will not be removed. The orthopedic injuries she has generally take from 6-8 months to heal.

What about healing of donor site? Dr. Mellissinos, her Plastic Surgeon at Hermann Professional Building, needs to see this site as he successfully deals with donor sites and their healing process routinely.

Dr. Tucker wanted to see Joyce in one month and scheduled appointment for 2/22 at 10:00. He wrote on back of appointment card that patient is to be transported by ambulance to appointments and ambulance staff to remain with patient. Should consider bringing additional pain medication from Beacon as he cannot provide.

When asked if she will walk again, Dr. Tucker said he definitely believes she will walk but she has a lot of pain and therapy ahead. Joyce is doing well. With the physical therapy she will receive, she should be much stronger when he sees her in a month.

*

Joyce attempts to arrange a meeting with Dr. Tucker while I try to meet with him at the same time. The following is Joyce's email to me:

DEAR RANDY,

I have an appointment with Dr. Tucker on September 7 at 10:00. I will get you the address. Do you just come with me and I bring a release?

I also have an appointment set up with Dr. Dholakia for the same day but at 2:00. I could not get it any closer to Dr. Tucker's appointment. Again, do I just bring a release?

I have a call into the UT to set up an appointment with Dr. Duke. I'm trying for the same day. I will send addresses later.

Joyce

I send emails to Dr. Tucker's academic administrator, Peggy, as well as one to the doctor:

PEGGY,

Please forward this to Dr. Tucker.
Thanks,
Randy Birken, MD

DR. TUCKER,

I have met with Dr. Ralph Lilly today and have finished my writing on Joyce's Memorial Hermann admission in 2000. Your input would be very helpful since so much of Joyce's surgeries were orthopedic.
Thanks,
Randy Birken, MD

PEGGY,

Please let Dr. Tucker know that I will be with Joyce Lance this Thursday. I had my receptionist reschedule my morning patients. Joyce will bring another patient release form. After Dr. Tucker sees Joyce, I'll ask him a few questions—don't want to hold up his office and I need to get back to mine as well. Maybe after we meet, he'll feel more comfortable with any further questions by email.
Thanks,
Randy Birken, MD

CHAPTER TWENTY-THREE

Meeting Dr. Tucker

UNLIKE THE MEETING WITH DR. LILLY, this time, the drive to the Texas Medical Center from North Houston is anything but smooth. The traffic snarls along I-45, the morning rush hour plus the relentless construction work. Added to my already tightened and frenetic day is a "fire" at my office; AT&T has interrupted the phones after twenty-seven years as a customer, a "problem" that they created with a cashed payment check from last month. "Just our policy, sorry," the customer rep says. Sorry? Turning off a physician's office phones is like severing the oxygen line to an underwater diver. Does the corporate world have a conscience, or is everything run by computer/data protocol? They agree to restore the phones "free of charge." Gee, thanks, I think, but I don't like my negative attitude. I need to transcend all my frustrations.

Dr. Tucker's office is in the same professional building as Dr. Lilly's, only this time, the parking lot is full. Fortunately, I find one vacant spot on the roof, but the elevators to the first floor are slow and ones to the eleventh floor are even slower. The time is ten minutes past ten o'clock—late, darn it. Rushing through the hallway, forehead now sweaty, the waiting room is just around the corner, a very different one than Dr. Lilly's; a large open room with rows of chairs lined up like a marching army, only the soldiers sitting in them are a mixture of casualties, not infantry. Crutches, braces, slings, casts, wheelchairs are their accoutrements, not firearms. A TV plays "Accent Health dot com" a continuous infomercial about surgical procedures and new treatments interspersed with pharmaceutical ads from asthma to erectile dysfunction, idealistic looking actors who appear happy and content after popping the drug company's pills. No one in the waiting room is watching, just background noise of no consequence.

Joyce is sitting near the back wall, a friendly smile and hug greet.

"I was worried when you weren't here at ten, so I called your office," she says softly and without judgment.

The morning is explained and Joyce gestures with her trademark nod, a simple, delicate one, acknowledging understanding and acceptance. Finally, relaxation sets in after the stressed out morning—could it be Joyce's equanimity that is the cure? I put my observation cap on, and scan the room for a personality, something that gives it flavor. On the wall is a framed poster of Michelangelo's "The Creation of Man" next to a botanical painting of a tree, the description too far away to read. The walls are paneled with dark wood, the carpet a neutral gray, and the words "UT Physicians, Orthopaedics" in large letters sits above. Why orthopaedics instead of orthopedics? Classier? More dignified? Close by is a bookcase with vintage medical texts: *Fractures, Dislocations, and Sprains*; *Regional Orthopedic Surgery*; *The Biochemistry and Physiology of Bone*. My reverie is interrupted by Joyce's voice.

"Did I ever show you what Dr. Tucker did to my legs?"

"No," I answer sheepishly, "I read about it in your hospital chart, but we never have discussed it."

"Right here," she points, "is where he attached the fixator." She smiles. "I didn't have enough bone left in my tibia, just a nubbin. So he had to hold everything together with an external appliance. I have a rod for my femur bone."

Ouch. Having sustained a broken leg from a skiing accident, the thought of bone pain elicits deep visceral unpleasant memories. A nubbin for bone? How does she walk?

"Here is where Dr. Tucker rebuilt my left leg, but he wasn't sure if I would need a knee replacement at a later day." Another classic Joyce smile. "He was right. That's when he referred me to another doctor for a knee replacement at Methodist Diagnostic Hospital about a year later."

Didn't know that and didn't know there was another ortho-
pedist involved with her rebuilding. Methodist?

"No, not The Methodist Hospital, but Methodist Diagnostic
Hospital."

While University of Texas Health Science Center boasts Memorial Hermann as its flagship hospital, with M.D. Anderson as
its great cancer institution, Baylor College of Medicine, U.T.'s rival
medical school, has always bragged about The Methodist Hospital, the place that Dr. Michael Debakey made famous. Like some
marriages, the medical school and Methodist split up—funny
how politics and economics can interfere with the most revered
matches; but this was Methodist Diagnostic Center Hospital, not
The Methodist Hospital.

"Yes, and that's when I developed a postoperative staph infection and was rehospitalized at Methodist Diagnostic for almost
six weeks."

Lila had mentioned this, but it never fit the time frame well.
Now it made sense. Joyce recovered from her trauma, but required a knee replacement about a year later, only to fight for
her life again, this time a bacteria instead of a Jaguar as the cause,
faded leg scars as testaments. Joyce shows no anger, no self-pity
for her past; the appreciation for her physicians is obvious as she
sits erect waiting to see the man, as her father stated, who "put
her back together."

An older male patient sits across in a wheelchair and lifts
his "bad" left leg with his hands, slight grimace on his face, and
gently places it in a more comfortable position, jogging pants cut
open to accommodate a small nerve stimulator attached to the
upper thigh. From across the room, another patient leans back,
eyes closed, left arm secured in a sling. A toddler, tired and bored,
pulls at his mother's legs as she tries to entertain him with toys
and books. The office door opens and a father pushes a wheelchair
out into the waiting room. His teenager son sits with headphones
on a shaved head wearing a tee-shirt with the words, "In Loving
Memory" printed above a photo that cannot be seen; another auto
accident, he as the survivor and mother/sister/girlfriend as a fatal

victim? These patients carry more than orthopedic problems, but the weight of an incident, sum larger than the parts.

"Joyce Lance," yells the receptionist.

As on command, Joyce stands and the receptionist leans her head out, body protected like armor from the door.

"We need to speak with you for a minute," she says perfunctorily.

Need to speak to her? Why? Is there a problem with her insurance, a draconian system of bureaucratic red tape, onerous restrictions, and flagrant disregard for patient welfare, a business strictly concerned about its own financial health and little about its policyholders? I must stop this cynicism. Relax, I tell myself silently.

Joyce is back in the waiting room, sits, and turns. "That was the office manager." She pauses and slightly lifts her chin. "She says that Dr. Tucker doesn't have time to talk to you." She swallows hard. "Sorry."

Doesn't have time to talk? His academic administrator received the email days ago along with Joyce's signed release; why now, after arrangements were made, meetings changed, and patients rescheduled to accommodate this appointment, the meeting to greet the surgeon who skillfully put back together bones that were broken, smashed, split, and crushed, a miraculous reconstruction of Joyce's once healthy infrastructure?

"She gave me this card," Joyce says.

On it is the academics administrator's name and phone number.

"She said for you to call and arrange a teleconference with Dr. Tucker when he's not seeing patients."

Okay, yes, it's hard to do anything else when you have a room full of patients waiting to see you, the doctor, like the incessant pharmaceutical reps who come by the office in the middle of an overwhelming day filled with problem patients, hospital phone calls, and postoperative demands, only to have you sign a laptop acknowledging their presence, a virtual attendance sheet for their district managers, a confirmation that they have given you a bite-sized statement that their product is better than their competitors so you better prescribe it otherwise you're a loser as a doctor. Yes, that kind of intrusion is unwelcome; but this is Joyce, the lady that not only survived but radiates goodwill and inspiration, and her sidekick writer who happens to be your colleague, another physician.

Joyce smiles, a slight comfort. "I'll talk with him when I'm in there," she says confidently. "I'm sure he'll want to at least say hello."

Yes, Joyce is right again. Maybe this wasn't the right forum to meet Dr. Tucker, but none of the many emails or phone calls was returned. Yet, one email, from the academic administrator, confirms that Dr. Tucker consents to either a phone call or email to share his memory of Joyce. After many months of no response, Joyce decided to make an appointment and introduce her doctor/writer/friend/collaborator to this gifted surgeon. Five minutes? How about thirty seconds?

The receptionist calls Joyce's name again. She smiles and walks through the door into the clinic. Time to read, catch up on some medical journals while waiting for her return and, hopefully, meet Dr. Tucker after Joyce explains things in person. Maybe that's all it will take, once he remembers Joyce and hears from her, directly, the purpose of a book about her incident, recovery, and the need to share her personal epiphanies with others who face difficult times. No, don't be angry. Try to understand his situation, the stress he must deal with while taking care of patients.

Waiting isn't easy for anyone in the room. The toddler, more rambunctious than earlier, is bored and tired. A security guard walks into the room, one crutch awkwardly balancing his left leg, and sits across, staring, almost uncomfortably. Am I getting paranoid? Would they summon a security guard to feign an injury just in case there's a conflict? Naw, that's ridiculous, my mind is playing tricks on my vulnerable psyche. The man with the sling is awake and reading *People Magazine*: "Why Paul Left Heather" is printed on the front cover. Another woman talks to the mother of the toddler.

"It's just not fair to wait this long," she says angrily.

"I know," the mother replies. "We've been waiting for over two hours."

"I read in a magazine that nurse practitioners can see patients for minor things and problems, letting the doctor see the important ones. Then we wouldn't have to wait so long."

The mother jumps from her chair, chasing her little boy who is now running wild in the waiting room. "Wow, that would be nice," she says while grabbing junior's back shirt and adeptly, like a cowboy wrestling a steer, pulling him down, lifting him up, and swiftly carrying him back to his chair in less than five seconds, maybe a world record. It's not fair to wait this long to see a clinician for a very short time when medical insurance premiums continue to escalate with high deductibles, providing a delivery system that is seriously inadequate and producing disgruntled patients who, while remaining appreciative for the doctor's skills and knowledge and occasional compassion, must endure. There I go again—entering the "Misanthrope Zone." I've got to rise above this, I tell myself, only my intellect is not overriding my emotions very well.

Joyce comes from the clinic to the waiting room. It's now 12:15 P.M., over two hours from the scheduled appointment. She's smiling; has Dr. Tucker agreed to meet? First and more importantly, what did he say about Joyce?

"He said that I'm doing great, that I'm a miracle woman," she answers, broad proud smile across her face.

Yes, of course, and why wouldn't he? Ninety percent of your bones were maimed, and now you walk, play, and exercise, a testament to his skills and your tenacity, an acknowledgment that you deserve and cherish. She lowers her head.

"He told me that he didn't have time to talk to you, that he could only do it on his time, not during clinic," she says quietly. "I told him why we're writing this book, to help others."

Okay, understood, but to hear from the man, his perspective, his take, his feelings, that's what has impact and meaning.

Again, Joyce's demurring nod quells the anger.

"I told him all that, but he insisted on meeting you on his terms, a teleconference from his academic office and not from the clinic."

All right, yes, but several attempts have been made to do that without results, that's why the appointment.

She shakes her head slowly. "I know, but that's what he kept telling me, on his terms only. Sorry."

I nod and agree. I must accept this as a minor inconvenience. Surely, the trip to the medical center was necessary, now that Dr. Tucker knows, direct from Joyce, about the book, and why. Papers, briefcase, and laptop are gathered. Joyce is parked in the same lot, only a few floors below. Before leaving the waiting room, Joyce stops and points to a photo on the wall.

"That's him, that's Dr. Tucker," she says proudly.

Distinguished and focused come to mind. Don't be mad, I tell myself. It's not a personal snub. The fraternity of physicians, once honored and respected, has lost its foundation, like the medical system itself that prided on conscientiousness and dedication. Just a handshake from a colleague, a respectful hello, let's talk when I can, would have been sufficient. Is it hubris, fear of publicity, or just lack of time? Joyce's light and pleasant conversation is settling. How does she do it? Keep that composure, that unruffled poise and equilibrium?

"Well, thanks for coming down here," she says as the elevator door opens to her floor. A hug and goodbye and the adventure is over.

Time to reflect while driving back to the office. Learn from Joyce. Don't waste energy on anger. Or maybe Peter's philosophy will help: Life is really simple if you appreciate what you've got. The cell phone rings to Dr. Tucker's administrative manager's line, a pleasant recorded voice asks for a message. After the beep, I explain everything; too bad things didn't work out today. Dr. Tucker's clinical manager asked that a meeting be scheduled. Here is my office private line, personal cell phone number, and home number as well. Look forward to hearing from you. Thanks.

Several days later, Dr. Tucker's academic administrator phones the office. She apologizes for the aborted meeting with Dr. Tucker when Joyce came for her visit, but after further consideration, he doesn't feel comfortable talking about Joyce's medical history. Sorry, he's a real great doctor and good guy.

No, don't get angry, I think. Leaning back in my office chair and contemplation seem more appropriate. What would Joyce do? Another epiphany: understanding and forgiveness. It's all right. As Elmore said, "the doctor who put Joyce back together." That's all that matters. I gulp my soft drink, get up, and tend to patients.

Chapter Twenty-Four

Dr. Duke

Dr. Duke,

This is a follow-up email regarding your patient, Joyce Lance, who survived a serious auto-pedestrian accident in October, 2000. As a physician and writer, I am creating a non-fiction account of her recovery through interviews and review of medical records.

Your input about her time at Hermann would be welcomed and appreciated.

Could we talk by phone or meet at your office? I practice in Spring, TX but can come to the Medical Center.

Thanks,

Randy Birken, MD

Dr. Duke,

Randy and I have been talking by e-mail and in person for several months. I am so pleased that he is going to write this book. This is not about me—the runner who got run over. Randy and I agree that it is about using my experience as a way to communicate a special message of hope to individuals who have suffered some traumatic event—whether physical, emotional, financial or psychological. And the message is that "we all have it in us to deal with these tragedies/traumas" even if we don't believe that now. We all have it within us—we just need to use it when "bad stuff" happens.

I can never thank everyone enough who was involved in my recovery. I had a wonderful life before my accident and I have a wonderful life now.

Randy and I also agree that I do not want any mention of the individual who hit me. I do not want to cause any further "hurt" in her life, and I am grateful that she stopped and called 911.

I will release any records to Randy from my time in the Hermann Trauma Center as well as the doctors who were so critical and dedicated to saving my life. And I can do that in whatever the appropriate release document is required.

I treasure the picture that I have of you and myself because I know that you and all of the doctors made it possible for me to continue to enjoy life.

Joyce

*

Five days after the aborted visit with Dr. Tucker, the Medical Center calls again, this time to meet Dr. Red Duke. The jaded phrase, "does not need any further introduction" is inappropriate for this doctor, a Houston icon, proud Texas native son, and the nation's own cowboy doctor. James Henry Duke, Jr. grew up in central Texas learning life through hard work set upon a strong moral foundation. His values and discipline were rewarded with the Boys Scouts' highest achievement—Eagle Scout.

After graduation from Texas A&M in 1950 with a degree in Economics, he served as a commissioned officer in the 67th Medium Tank Battalion. After returning to Texas, he attended The University of Texas Southwestern Medical School in 1956 and completed his residency training in surgery at Parkland Memorial Hospital during the time President Kennedy was assassinated and brought to that institution's emergency room. With a curiosity for understanding the metabolic and physiological changes associated with trauma, he accepted a fellowship in research at Columbia University's College of Physicians and Surgeons. Four years later, he assisted in the formation of a new medical school in Afghanistan, moving his family there. He attended to surgical traumas ranging from major orthopedic injuries, to gun shot wounds, parasitic infections, as well as camel bites. After personal bouts with hepatitis and tuberculosis, he returned home to Texas to join the new faculty at the University of Texas Houston Medical School to continue research on surgical metabolism and nutrition; but clinical medicine called again, this time in 1976 when he commanded the trauma center at Hermann Hospital. Soon after, in 1978, the Life Flight Helicopter Service was formed, creating Houston's air ambulance, a service providing expert and expeditious trauma care to the country's fourth largest city. Dr. Duke's extraordinary efforts to educate the public about health issues, as well as his persistent dedication to the discipline of trauma medicine, brought him into strong consideration for Surgeon General of the United States in 1989. As a champion for environmental preservation, he has served as president of the Texas Bighorn Society, Foundation for North American Wild Sheep, as well as the Boone and Crockett Club, America's oldest conservation organization. As former host of the 1986-89 PBS series *Bodywatch*, Dr. Duke has been featured on several national news reports, health specials, and a television series. In 1988, he was named "Surgeon of the Year" by the James F. Mitchell Foundation.

His photos reveal incongruities: a lanky, bespectacled intellectual, comfortably wearing either a surgeon's cap or cowboy hat, either sitting at a desk or on a horse. A man driven for knowledge or education, he is both a renaissance man and a cowboy simultaneously—giving, protecting, and teaching with a frontier-style attitude that is unabashed and unpretentious. How ironic and fortuitous that this man of discipline, fortitude, and passion would be in charge of the trauma team when Joyce arrived at Hermann Hospital.

"I was so fortunate to have Dr. Duke care for me the morning of the accident. Lila told me what he said to her that evening."

Yes, the photo of her with Dr. Duke, as well as reading Lila's notes, indicates that Joyce was fortunate, although "fortunate" may not be the appropriate word. The waiting room is like the one in the orthopedic department, with the words "UT Physicians—General, Plastics, and Pediatric Surgery Center" on a distant wall, champagne-yellow paint contrasting with the burgundy carpet. Who does the interior decorating around here? Dr. Lilly, obviously more discerning, didn't accept the institutional styling and did his own thing, but the orthopedic and surgery department adminis-trators were not interested in the right color scheme—just a wait-ing room ma'am, the facts and nothing more. Interestingly, there is a faster pace here than over in the broken bone service; doors open magically from different parts of the room, like a fun house at an amusement park—people going in and coming out without any logic to it. What's the deal here? Is this a medical department or a three-ring circus?

Joyce is engaged in conversation with a man sitting near her, his animated voice and gesticulations passionate. He's talking about the sudden drop in gas prices and theorizes, in a convo-luted way, about corporate monopoly and global shenanigans. Joyce listens intently, politely, never intimating disinterest or disrespect—that's Joyce—prim and diplomatic, caring and com-passionate. Suddenly, the man's name is called and he stands and nods, a non-verbal communication acknowledging thanks. Joyce's inimitable smile reciprocates kindness and peace. A TV above is tuned to CNN. Where is Accent Health dot com? Still, no one is watching. A nurse announces Joyce's name. She stands erect, deliberately holding onto her purse and briefcase, and gives a reassuring stare. Will Dr. Duke do the same as Dr. Tucker?—re-fuse to see the person writing about her accident and recovery? She takes a deep breath, smiles, and walks into the clinic.

A young man with crutches walks into the waiting room. Hey, bud—the orthopods are on the eleventh floor, not the four-teenth. He sits, grabs a magazine, and waits—waits like all the other patients, family, and friends, an annoying part of one's life, as distasteful as being stuck in a traffic jam or waiting in line at the motor vehicle department, a fact of life that, unfortunately, remains a traditional, aggravating, part of our medical delivery system: medical histories, insurance cards, co-pays, and the end-less forms of attorney-induced disclaimers that you, the patient, must sign, otherwise you don't get any help; worthless defense forms that you agree to, hostage-like, that you indemnify with a signature not to sue or harass as well as honoring unexpected expenses, so help you God, otherwise the unscrupulous credit agency will bug you until you cry uncle for privileged medical care provided graciously. Who wants to be sick or have a medical problem? Who wants to sit and wait and be given a two-minute evaluation and a diagnosis coupled with outrageously expensive prices? You wait for all this? But there is little other choice; of course you want a well-trained medical doctor, years of scientific training and clinical acumen, a man or woman who has spent anywhere from twelve to fifteen years post-high school, a person burdened to see as many patients as possible to compensate for insurance reimbursements that are lower than twenty years ago, escalating malpractice premiums created by avaricious personal injury attorneys, questions about direct-to-consumer ads for a drug company's pill du jour, selfish patients who abuse the system when not accountable for their demands, and medical societies, pressured by the lawmakers, requiring unrealistic continuing medical education credits to appease public perception. A good system? Naw, but it's all that's out there, at least for now. So you sit and wait after signing forms that you haven't read, and hope that the visit will alleviate your problem or problems.

Suddenly, I spot another room, way in the back of the larger waiting area. A fish tank, bubbly water with shiny fish swimming through artificial reefs, stones, and gravel strategically built into the wall to be seen from within as well from the outside. What is this and what is on the other side of this fish tank? Casual inspection reveals something unexpected—it's a pediatric surgical waiting room. I glance through the fish tanks and see mother and kids, parents and kids, and probably grandparents and kids—little ones with bandages, catheters, and IV's. My previous anger and cynicism is superseded by empathy. These young patients don't want to be here either, preferring to be outdoors playing with friends, indoors watching TV or intrigued with a video game, puzzle, or whatever kind of pretend creativity is imagined. *There* is the answer. Patients wait and wait because of a common denominator—hope—hope to feel better, be normal, free of the worry. Slumping back in my chair, it becomes apparent. A disorganized, tarnished medical system? Yes, but one that addresses a basic emotion as well—fear. So waiting is accepted, although dreaded, for the possible reassurance as well as peace of mind. It's a draconian, twisted, and unjust system, but all so human.

Joyce appears from the clinic; a hesitant smile greets me. Is Dr. Duke willing? Joyce shakes her head.

"I'm afraid he's not here today."

"What?"

"He's out of town, so another doctor, his godson, saw me and apologized for the confusion." She gazes downward. "So I have to make another appointment to see Dr. Duke." The smile returns. "His godson was very kind."

Another roadblock? No, not really, actually a step closer to the man, the cowboy doctor, Dr. Red Duke, trauma surgeon deluxe, the man who brought Joyce back to life. There is a return date; then, the elusive ubermensch/doctor will be met. All is well in waiting, for there is always hope.

CHAPTER TWENTY-FIVE

Dr. Duke Redux

OKAY, TODAY'S THE DAY. It's been several weeks since the aborted visit with the famed Dr. Red Duke, and Joyce's rescheduled appointment is at 1 PM. With the dry run completed, nothing should interfere with this anticipated meeting, a chance to see a celebrity in person, to interact with Joyce and one of her saviors, an opportunity to greet a surgeon with true grit, salt-of-Texas earth, a man of principle, dedication, and demands worthy of vintage medicine and, when doctoring was cherished by practitioners, untainted by insurance, malpractice, and politics.

With the afternoon clinic rescheduled, patient calls returned, and post-ops discharged from the hospital, only the meeting with Dr. Duke and Joyce remains, except for a three o'clock meeting near the Galleria. How much time could Dr. Duke spend with Joyce? Probably only a few minutes to say hi, shake her hand, and discuss the miraculous recovery, followed by a hug and return to seeing his afternoon patients—maybe I'll have time for a latte before that three o'clock meeting. While Fannin Street was crowded, the normally full parking lot next to the UT Physicians office building had empty spots. It felt good not to be rushed—this is the way to live—being productive without additional time burdens. Life without stress should be cherished.

Last time, Joyce sat near the TV in the large waiting room, but a quick glance around revealed empty chairs and no Joyce on the radar screen. Was it too early, the wrong time, certainly not the wrong day? The receptionist smiles, a reassurance, and says that

Joyce has already been brought back to an exam room. What? No! It was only 12:45 PM. This couldn't be.

"That's okay," she says cheerily. "You can go back there. Just go through the door to the left."

You have to be kidding. Don't you want to know who I am before letting me enter the clinic? The antithesis to the orthopedic department—casualness almost bordering on complacency; but it felt right. Why not? Why should there be burdensome restrictions and red tape? Heck, these guys are trauma surgeons when the difference between life and death is fragile seconds, or millimeters below or above vital organs. So you say you're with the patient—no problem—welcome. Joyce is alive, that's all that matters. Go back, be with her, and enjoy every moment of her existence, when six years ago, her lungs and circulation were mechanically controlled, and her brain, perhaps asleep, was not functioning. Yes, this was the way it should be—don't sweat the small stuff when it comes to a trauma survivor—nothing else after that is quite that serious.

The clinic hallway is light and austere compared to the dark and stuffy, albeit poorly decorated, waiting room, more like a hospital corridor than an office. Two nurses sit at a centered desk.

"Joyce Lance?" one said. "Sure, she's in room one, just down the hall."

Unbelievable. Just like the receptionist. Okay, yes, down the hall in room one, gotcha', sure, thanks.

"Come in." Joyce's voice is strong and clear. She sits on an armless chair near an outdated exam table, circa nineteen fifty-ish. The room is more acetic than the hallway, an otoscope and opthalmoscope perched above the table, a few unframed charts tacked to the walls—"The Digestive System," "The Head," and "The Abdomen" grace faded white walls. No frills here. If you're breathing, that's all that matters; accoutrements and adornments are unnecessary when the human machine is alive and well. A window straight ahead frames a large air conditioning duct on the roof next door; but to Joyce's left is another window, this one showcasing Rice University's intimate campus where stately academic buildings are caressed by large green trees. In the distance is Rice Stadium, home of Super Bowl VIII, an inviting football facility, symbolizing the amalgam of the collegiate gridiron with the pursuit of academic excellence and intellectual erudition. Houston is proud of this prestigious institution, dubbed the Harvard of the South, a university blending small student classes with internationally renowned faculty, a place where one Ivy League trained professor confided that "this is the greatest school to teach at." Ironically, Rice University and the Texas Medical Center are neighbors, a contrast between urban verve and vitality and the insulated, protected environment of esteemed higher education. While patients are treated in the clinics, hospitals, and surgical suites, students learn and research not only higher technology, but the refinement of intellectual quest and edification.

Joyce looks great, again much younger appearing than her fifty-eight years. Paradoxically, the conversation is light and pleasant while sounds of voices, machines, and keyboards, products of a medical office, radiate from the hallway. It's 1:15. Is that Dr. Duke outside the room, talking to house officers and medical students, his gruff Texas twang spewing medical knowledge, relevant and enlightening? No one enters, and Joyce talks about her precious grandchildren, Ally and Clay, and how Don's blood pressure is under control. Talk like old friends or family—maybe that's what it should be by now, learning about her life without barriers or disguises, a woman who believes in herself as well as her role in this world, undaunted and undisturbed. Neither one watches much TV; book imagery is the entertainment. Days of running, history for both Joyce and I, hers related to trauma, mine to damaged Achilles' tendons, now becomes a topic, fond memories of a glorious sport/meditation vital to existence as eating and sleeping.

Joyce smiles, "Oh, I didn't tell you. Peter's engaged."

"To Meghan?" I ask excitedly.

"Yes."

Great. They appeared to be a good fit.

Joyce nods, her trademark gesture indicating acceptance without conditions.

More activity just outside the exam room. It must be Dr. Duke. Joyce is in her ever-present state of calm contrasted with my sweaty palms confirming my anxiety. I glance at my watch—1:40. Heck, plenty of time. He'll be here soon. But I keep thinking about that meeting at 3 PM. Joyce talks about work, but one of my ears is glued to the hall sounds.

I'm too antsy and must check it out. I excuse myself, leave the room, and walk to the nurses' station and ask about Dr. Duke to an unnerved person.

"Oh," she says matter-of-factly, "Dr. Duke is never on time."

But it's almost two o'clock," I ask, surprised at my whiny intonation.

A male nurse snorts. "Hey, you never know when he's going to show up."

Hmmm. Hands seem sweatier. A nurse practitioner understands.

"I'll call the OR and check on him."

The OR? No! Well, yes he's a surgeon, and anything can happen, but he has clinic at one. Suddenly, a realization is made—this isn't the world of private practice, something familiar to me for the past twenty-seven years; this is the academic life and different terms exist here.

"Uh-huh. Okay, great." She hangs up and smiles.

"He's finishing up. Be down in ten minutes."

Whew, okay, relax now, I tell myself. I go tell Joyce and our conversation continues; talk of Pilates and hiking, and authors like Wally Lamb, John Wooden, and T.C. Boyle. I don't want to look at my watch, but I do and cringe when I see 2:15. I leave the room and ask the nurse again.

"I'll call again," the pleasant nurse practitioner says. "Hello, oh, hello Dr. Duke."

Darn, she's talking to him.

"Yes, well we have clinic patients." She listens. "Yes, they were scheduled at one."

Oh my gosh, he forgot about clinic! It's 2:25! What to do?

"He said he'll be here in about ten minutes."

No, no. Can't wait, got to be at that meeting. A deflated walk back to Joyce's exam room. She takes the news in typical stride.

"Please, Joyce," I ask beseechingly, "send me an email tonight. And tell Dr. Duke I'm sorry. Okay?"

She nods that famous comforting gesture. It's okay. I must accept this. But why again? An opportunity lost or a gift in disguise?

Time for latte? Heck, with the construction on Woodway near Memorial, near where Joyce was hit by the Jaguar, nothing is calm and unrushed. Darn, I wanted to shake that great man's hand, see him in person, his wide bushy mustache covering his upper lip while he talks, clear eyes narrowed and focused, the assertiveness of a quarterback, the confidence of Lance Armstrong, the energy of an athlete. No, it must be learned through Joyce's words. That's okay—that's what Joyce would say and believe. Her attitude is a gift to all who know her.

*

Randy,

Dr. Duke and his PA came to see me a little before 3:00. I explained who I was and showed him the picture from when I had met him before. Back in April, he was very busy with patients and I did not stay for more than seven or eight minutes. Even when he had a hectic schedule, he seemed very interested in me and how I "had turned out." He asked me about running. I told him I was not running anymore, but was doing Pilates, the treadmill, the elliptical and, when I have the opportunity, hiking. He invited me to come to see him again when he had more time.

In April he had his famous red handkerchief around his head. Today, he had an army/military camouflage cap with cloth extensions to tie it on the back of his head.

He sat down on his stool and said that he had been in surgery. It was a pedestrian/automobile accident which required some major efforts to stop the bleeding and will require more surgery to close the wound. I felt like I was taking time that would be better utilized with patients such as the one mentioned above, but he was very patient and ready to hear how I was doing. He said that he sees patients on Mondays only and is in surgery, etc. for the rest of the week.

He asked me about work and what I am doing. I told him that I had returned to my same job at Klein Bank. I emphasized that all of the people that I work with were so wonderful to "do my job" until I could return to the bank. My bosses, John Klein and Michael Brummerhop, were so supportive of me and my son during this time. I cannot say how grateful I am to everyone at Klein Bank for making it possible to return to my job. And while I was in the rehabilitation center, they never let me feel like I had left the "outside world."

After I left the rehabilitation center, my son, Peter, took care of me day and night so I did not have to go to an assisted living center. That meant so much to me!

I thanked Dr. Duke for being the coordinator of my stay at the trauma center at Hermann Hospital. I know that my accident was awful, but I also am so grateful for my life, my son and grandchildren, Don, my family and friends and my co-workers.

I told Dr. Duke that if I had not been in Houston and had the wonderful and dedicated medical care that I had, there might not have been a happy ending. I also told him that I have read so much about his contributions to the medical field, especially life flight and trauma care.

I said that I know that I am one of many people he has seen in the trauma center, but that I could not thank him enough for what he had done for me. He said that it is always nice to see positive results and to hear the words—"thank you."

He said that he and Hermann Hospital work with a lot of "blunt trauma" patients versus patients that have been shot, etc. He said that I was definitely a blunt trauma patient and that my good health had helped me live. He said that he and his staff can help with the medical remedies of accidents, etc., but that it is then up to the patient as to what they do with their life.

I showed him the pictures of my grandchildren, Ally and Clay, and told him that my son and grandchildren make my life absolutely worth every second. I am so blessed to have had such great support and friendship, be in the right place with regards to medical treatment, and that I must have known I still had a wonderful life ahead of me and did not want to leave.

As I left, I again thanked him. He shook my hand and said that I looked like I was doing well. When I opened the door to leave, he said, "Okay, Grama, enjoy those children."

Joyce

CHAPTER TWENTY-SIX

Michael Brummerhop— Bank President and CEO

JUST TWO SURGERIES INTO THE MORNING—three more to go. Quick cup of coffee and a glance at the clock—its 11 A.M. and my meeting with Michael Brummerhop, the President and CEO of the former Klein Bank, one of the top executives Joyce worked with, is scheduled for 12:45 P.M. By the time I finish my surgeries, there'll be no time to meet with him. Reluctantly, I call my receptionist and ask her to call his administrative secretary.

"Tell her that my first surgery took three hours instead of the planned one." I sigh disappointedly.

Bad luck? Zilch with Dr. Tucker, a missed opportunity with Dr. Duke, and now this. Maybe he can meet after office patients today.

It's three o'clock and a large stack of charts sit on the desk sticking its tongue out at me like Dennis the Menace to Mr. Wilson. Tired and spent from the morning's surgeries, I see the office fires as an uncontrolled forest conflagration.

What did Michael Brummerhop say?

The office receptionist is buried deep in work and answers without looking up. "He can't meet. He had a problem at his ranch, had to leave, and won't be back for a few weeks."

A few weeks! No! Another missed chance to speak to one of Joyce's close allies. Can't wait that long.

"Do me a favor. Call his administrator. See if I can call him at his ranch or at least email him."

"Okay," she says perfunctorily.

I tell myself to get it together and get my mind focussed on work. One patient with a positive breast biopsy—call her first; an ultrasound report showing large fibroid tumors; and an endless stack of abnormal Pap smears, low bone-density scans, and an array of patient questions regarding hormones, vaginal infections, irregular bleeding, and anxiety/depression problems—the usual things, at times common to a medical staff, but of utmost concern and priority to the patient.

An hour later, the receptionist puts mail on my desk.

Did you find out anything about Michael Brummerhop?

"Oh, yeah. His administrator left him a message on his cell. There's no land line at his ranch and he doesn't have email access." She smiles sympathetically.

Thanks. Probably never get to talk with him.

How would Joyce handle this? She'd probably nod reassuringly and say, if it was meant to be, then he'd call. Think like that, think with composure, acceptance, and without irritation. Yeah, keep trying.

Just before five, the phone intercom rings.

"Michael Brummerhop's on line three."

What? Charts fall on the floor while I lunge for the phone.

"Sorry we missed each other." His voice is deep and his accent thickly Texan. "I'm calling from a little café, so if you hear trucks rolling by, you'll know why." His hearty laugh drowns out the loud background noises.

Tell me about Joyce, as a worker and person.

"Well," he says deliberately. "Joyce is more than an employee; she's a friend as well."

Nothing new. He continues.

"Without a doubt, Joyce is the brightest and hardest working person ever employed by me. I'll tell you, when she got hurt, I had my doubts about her recovery. I mean, not about surviving, but functioning like she used to. But she's the same old Joyce before her accident—smart and with unmatched work ethics."

Another confirmation.

"God knows that after having almost all your bones broken, in a coma for weeks, and then all that awful rehab, I'd been darn depressed. I mean, who wouldn't?" He pauses as the sounds of an eighteen-wheeler rolls by. "Heck, not Joyce. Nope. The same sweet woman who everyone loves. I'm telling you, she's one of a kind."

Chicken scratch scribble on the back of a medical journal captures his comments.

"You know, Joyce and I used to run together at Memorial. I'd do my ten miles and she'd do her six, except on the weekends when she'd do her long runs. I ran some short ones, but not those 26'ers she did."

Don't want to hold him up. He was kind enough to call.

"I've worked with hundreds of people in my life; no one, I mean no one, is quite like her."

Chapter Twenty-Seven

Joyce

October 7, 2006

In just a few days it will be six years since my accident. October 20, 2000. I do not look back at this date as the day that negatively changed my world. I look at October 20, 2000 and then I look at October 20, 2001, 2002, 2003, 2004, 2005 and 2006—it is six years since I "got run over" and I am alive and doing well!

Albeit, I do not run marathons, or even run, but I continue my enjoyment for working out and exercise. I do Pilates, walk, treadmill, and use the elliptical machines regularly. And when I have the opportunity, I love to hike. Don and I have hiked Muir Woods in San Francisco, Yosemite National Park, Acadia National Park, and other places at which we have vacationed. I use hiking sticks because I am uncertain of the terrain, but it is so refreshing and I enjoy the beautiful outside.

Klein Bank was bought by Amegy Bank of Texas after I returned to work. The people I worked with at Klein Bank were the greatest people ever! Now I work with a wonderful company/ people at Amegy Bank as an Area Manager. Many of my fellow Klein Bank employees now are great employees of Amegy Bank! Another change in my life, but one I embrace and am dedicated to.

My son is engaged to be married to a wonderful person, Meghan Lyons. Meghan deeply loves Peter's children, Allyson and Clay. I love to go to their gymnastics and swimming classes each week. Allyson and Clay have attended Lakewood Montessori School in Houston since they were babies, and this wonderful school—its owners and teachers—have had a very positive affect on my two grandchildren—a great school with a long waiting list!

Don is my "soul mate" of many years and is wonderful. I am so blessed to have someone as loving as Don. He is so wise—a great person who reads extensively and can see many sides of any topic or issue. He has the amazing ability to know when I "need" to do something for myself and when I need his help. I love him so much!

And certainly there is my family. My mother passed away about two years ago, but my mother and father, and my sisters and brother were there and supporting me. I have been the "daughter on the phone" for most of my years, because I have not lived in Minnesota for a very long time. My sisters, brother, and Mom and Dad called me frequently. My mom and dad came down to Houston after I left the rehabilitation center. My sister, Kathy, came down several times and later came to Houston with my father after my mother had passed away. My brother, Ken, and his wife, Alice, also came to see me. My mother, who was living at the time, told me that I absolutely could not be in the hospital when they came. I disappointed her as I had a knee replacement and developed a staph infection. She understood and "forgave me." Ken and Alice came to the hospital, which was wonderful.

I cannot say enough about the people I worked with at Klein Bank. John Klein, the Chairman of the Board and Michael Brummerhop, the President and CEO, were so supportive during my recovery and made it possible that I could return to the bank in the same position that I was in prior to my accident. They kept me involved with what was happening at the bank and encouraged the people that I worked with to help me "see outside of Beacon."

My managers of the twenty-eight Klein Bank branches and their employees visited me frequently. Connie Taylor, the banking center manager at Old Town Spring and also part of my Branch Administration group, came before she went to work and brought me breakfast. Later in the day, she brought me a high protein drink from Smoothie King. Naomi Kleb, banking center manager at Tomball Parkway and also part of my Branch Administration group, took on a lot of my responsibilities and called and visited me frequently. Not only were they there for me, but also for Peter. What wonderful people!

Jennifer Pittman, banking center manager at Steeplechase and part of Branch Administration, who was also the expert on in-store banking, was an important part of the team that assumed my responsibilities while I was recovering. She also helped Peter during my time at Hermann Hospital.

Peter said that he could not believe I had been in such a serious accident and the decisions he was being asked to make. He also said he was amazed at the number of "important people" at the hospital. He really sought and took the advice of many of my Klein Bank friends as well as the doctors at Hermann Hospital and at the Beacon Rehabilitation Center.

Allyson was amazing. She was born on August 29, 2000. When she and her dad visited me at Beacon, she would sit on my bed and not move as if she knew it would hurt me. When Peter took me to the Medical Center for appointments after I left Beacon, Allyson would sit in my lap while Peter pushed the wheel chair. She was like a porcelain doll—again, it seemed she sensed that it would hurt me if she moved.

I will say that my recovery was a very physically painful time for me. It seemed as if my life had changed overnight. (Not so. I was at Hermann from October 20, 2000, until I arrived at Beacon on November 13 of the same year, but I do not remember anything until I arrived at Beacon.) Maybe because I did not know and did not ask about the seriousness of my accident, I could only think about getting better and getting back to my family, friends and work. I never believed I wouldn't walk. I never believed I wouldn't return to my "life before the accident." And because I felt so, I knew the pain was a necessary part of my recovery. While at Beacon, I recall trying to negotiate with God. If he would just let me go home for a few days and be like I was prior to my accident, I would come back and finish my therapy, etc.

Many people have told me that I should write a book about my experiences to help others. I started to do so and in five years I completed three chapters. I felt that I could help people on a one-on-one basis. I am also very averse to being the center of attention.

When attending an appointment with Dr. Gary Urano, we talked about me writing a book. He encouraged me and asked if he could have Dr. Randy Birken contact me. Randy has written books and has had them published. Dr. Urano asked for my e-mail address so that Dr. Birken could contact me.

Randy and I e-mailed back and forth in the latter months of 2005. I sent him my three chapters. We began to talk and I knew that he was the person to help me help others by writing this book. I know so today.

Randy has met with my Klein Bank friends, Peter, the EMS person at my accident scene (Matthew Sultemeier), Dr. Ralph Lilly, my friend Lila Hammann, Don, and my long-time high school friend, Connie Bock in Minnesota. While in Minnesota, he met and visited with my dad, and brother and sister-in-law. And certainly we have discussed or met with the many doctors who were there to help me—Dr. Red Duke, Dr. Jeffrey Tucker, and Dr. Ralph Lilly.

Since the beginning, my purpose has been to help people deal with "bad stuff." I am the individual who ran 45 to 65 miles per week. At the same time, I am the person who refused flu shots and did routine doctor visitations reluctantly. I am not the center of this book. I am not what this book is about. This book is about how one day "everything is OK" and the next day everything has changed, and how we deal with it. We may believe we do not have the inner strength to deal with a traumatic event, but that strength is deep within us all if we choose to use it.

Many people have said that they could not have "done what I did." My response is, "if your choices are to die, be an invalid, or get up and get on with life—what would you choose?"

I know that my determination was a critical part, but I also know that everything and everyone else was part of what made it possible for me to live and continue my life. Everything is not as it was before. Some parts of me are "numb," and my knees do not bend like they did before. I was right-handed and now I am left-handed. But I am alive and still have wonderful friends, my Minnesota family, Peter/Meghan and Ally and Clay. I have the most wonderful man in my life, Don Larson. And Dr. Randy Birken has been an amazing beacon in my life to help me help others through his words.

Randy has asked that I look in retrospect at my accident, recovery, and the many people that we have talked to in the course of writing this book. He is an insightful person and I am so glad he is writing this book.

As we have talked with people, such as Connie Taylor, Naomi Kleb, Jennifer Pittman, Lynell Brooks, Rhonda Krahn and Gloria Ewert, whom I had worked with at Klein Bank, I knew the seriousness of my accident. When Randy and I met with these special people, I also knew that I had been very close to death. I knew this, yet had not experienced what they had during this time. They carried the burden and pain for me while I was lying unconscious at Hermann Hospital.

My dear friend, Lila, and I talked several times about how I was "missing," became Jane Doe, and was found at the Hermann Hospital Trauma Center. It was very painful for Lila and many times we cried with each other. I guess, because it was so hurtful for Lila, I did not want to talk about it with my family and friends/co-workers. When Randy met with my friends, I learned a lot about what happened and saw how hurtful it was for them

Gloria Ewert has been a wonderful part of everything I do at Amegy Bank. She works with all of the fantastic employees in our market area. I remain surrounded by special people.

to recall it also. Peter joined us for the get together and left after a while since he was not ready at that time to remember what had happened.

Peter was a "rock" for me and always working to make sure I had the best care while raising his infant daughter. I could not have asked for a more wonderful son even if I had been able to "pick him off the shelf." Allyson was always a delight to see. There is something special about a son and granddaughter. And in January, 2003, Ally's baby brother, Clay, joined the family. They are so special to me. Ally will explain to Clay when I cannot go as fast as they go, that "Grama hurt her legs" and that they need to wait for me.

And looking back on this whole "race for life," I realize that all of the pain and uncertainty while I was at Hermann was borne by others as well. I was unconscious. I feel badly that I caused such sorrow and uncertainty for everyone in my life. I became aware of this during the writing of this book and the meetings with people.

When I read things like, "She was either going to be alive when she reached Hermann Hospital or she would be a good organ donor," a big lump gathered in my throat. When Randy met with Dr. Lilly and his first question was, "Is she still alive?" I felt the same emotion.

Another thing I learned about myself was that I did not want people who cared for me to see that I was in pain. I was sure that no one could see my fixator, casts, bandages, etc. by keeping my covers up to my neck. I could do nothing about hiding my halo, however. I knew people were worried for me and I did not want to add to that worry.

A psychiatrist worked with me during this recovery time, to help me control the pain. I learned to take my mind to "a different place" when the pain was great. This is not a foreign concept when running marathons. This transference of pain mindset was a big help.

Probably the biggest thing I learned about myself was that I was used to being the strong person. I wanted to help and liked helping other people. I had always felt I was self-sufficient and very independent. Suddenly, I could not move anything without help. I could not feed myself and had to have someone hold the phone to my ear so I could talk. I was flat on my back for over five months because of the fixator and halo.

I saw how all of the wonderful people in my life wanted to help me and do things for me that I could not do. I was lying in bed with my hair the color of a snowball and my teeth were all damaged. I would have never allowed myself to be seen like this by anyone. I always wore makeup and took care in how I dressed and did my hair. Still trying to hide my injuries, I realized how many wonderful people were doing everything for me, and I appreciated it greatly. I willingly accepted their help and knew that they did it because they cared for me.

Peggy Coleman, a business development officer at Klein Bank, now Amegy Bank, took me to physical therapy three times a week when I had returned to work in my wheelchair and could not

In 2007, I fell in love with the photos of Connor and Theo, my dear pomeranians. They were born on Finch Island in Washington state and flew to Houston as puppies to keep my life young.

walk. She folded up the wheelchair after helping me get in the car with my sliding board and then reversed the whole process when she came to pick me up three hours later. Connie Taylor rode with me on many trips by ambulance to my doctors' appointments in the Medical Center. I cannot write about all of the wonderful things that people have done for me.

Still today, people will carry things for me, bring me food while I'm at work, help me put on necklaces I can't clasp myself, and help me up and down curbs. The list is endless. I know that my accident and all of the people involved in my recovery have made me a person who is still very self-sufficient, but also one that can give more of myself to others and let them help me. I can help them back in other ways.

People ask me if I'm angry about my accident and how it changed my life. I have no anger. I had a great life before and I have a great life now. I do not know why this happened to me, but I don't see it as a punishment, fate or anything like that. I believe it just happened. I do not plan to spend the rest of my life trying to figure any of this out. I want to continue to have a wonderful life, and one way I can do so is to help others who experience something catastrophic in their lives. It can be physical, mental, the death of a loved one, a disease, financial problems, divorce, etc. And when these types of things happen to us, in our minds they are huge. When people talk to me about something happening in their lives, many times they will stop themselves and say that they should not complain, because what is happening to them is nothing compared to what happened to me. I always tell them that if it is big in their lives, then it is big. It doesn't matter what happened to me. I want to help them and I think I can do so to a greater extent today than I could six years ago.

So my longest marathon and my fight for survival are in most aspects over. What I do with the rest of my life is up to me, and I plan to live a happy life surrounded by wonderful people with whom I can share life.

CHAPTER TWENTY-EIGHT

Last Meeting

JOYCE'S LIVING ROOM IS COMFORTABLE AND COZY; tranquil new age piano music gently permeates the air, a noticeable contrast to the previous meeting with Peter, Meghan, and Joyce's grandkids. That time, the late afternoon sunlight was hot and irritating, mixed with distractingly edgy TV sounds. Joyce looks good, a cup of chamomile tea and a hard cover book sit next to her. If a fluffy long-haired cat were sleeping on her lap, the scene would be idyllic and postcard perfect.

"I love my chamomile tea. I drink it all day," she says with her trademark grin.

The laptop boots up noisily. This is the last meeting between subject and writer, the end of a series that began less than a year ago when little was known other than the miraculous survival of a marathon runner from a near fatal trauma. Is there nervousness present? Not really; both participants seem calm and accepting, although the research into Joyce's accident, past and present, was anything but halcyon. Courage was required by most inter-viewed, a need to dig up buried memories, remembrances of a human drama among family and friends. Was it worth it?

Joyce nods. "Certainly. If it can help others overcome personal obstacles, yes, definitely."

Did you, personally, gain anything?

"Oh, yes. No one had discussed what went on when I was in my coma." She bows her head deftly. "I wish I hadn't caused so much pain to them."

Pain?

"Yes, their worry about me. I didn't want them to hurt."

Unselfish and humble as usual, Joyce never focuses on herself—it's always about others.

"Well, I knew what I had to do and that was to get better and get back to my life. It was clear to me. Everyone was so supportive and caring ... that I appreciate. But I didn't want them to worry about me. I knew what I had to do."

She gets up and walks to the kitchen, presumably to prepare healthy snacks. Her style is predictable now, proper graciousness a part of her persona.

Her living room is familiar, chairs that embrace, simple yet elegant furniture, functional and stylish, an ambrosial view of tall pines and verdant grass. It's Joyce's home and it feels right—an extension of her calming self. She returns with a tray of ripe fruit, aged cheese, and those famous healthy crackers. Chamomile tea does seem appropriate. She continues as if she never left the room.

"I was busy going ahead with life, trying to recover." She pauses. "But now I understand the emotional intensity for everyone else." She shakes her head solemnly. "I never wanted to be the only topic, you know, having people dwell on me."

Dwell?

"Yes, you see, we all must get over bad things and get on with our lives," she says, hands gesticulating rhythmically. "I needed to get back to my routine, even at Beacon. John and Mike recognized that, so they kept me involved with the bank business ... using my cell phone, laptop, teleconferences." She delicately sips her tea. "It was good not to lose that, you know, to stay busy. It helped me survive and not focus on my pain."

Joyce sighs quietly. It is a rare moment of an uncomfortable memory.

"I anticipated pain and I knew when I was going to hurt, but as time went on, my body got used to it ... kind of like running a marathon. Ten miles to go ... so learn how to displace the pain." She smiles. "I still do that today, when I hike, when I go to work, everything. The psychologist at Beacon worked with me. Well, I already knew about how to do it, but his suggestions helped."

How?

She nods. "Well, it's like mental exercise where you learn to go to another place where the pain isn't as bad."

"You mean some kind of transcendental meditation?" I ask curiously, although not surprised Joyce would practice it.

She shakes her head.

"No, I wouldn't call it just meditation. You have to learn how to do it, practice it." Her head tilts to the side. "Well, maybe it's meditative, but I look at it as a skill I learned while training for marathons ... miles to go and things hurt, so you bump into something painful and just bounce off and run around it and refocus." Another patrician smile. "I use that technique for everything in life ... you hit a wall, get up, and get going again."

Fingers pause before hitting the laptop keys. "When did you learn to do this?"

Joyce narrows her lips contemplatively. "You know, I think it was defined by how I grew up. We had chores before and after school and homework to do before TV." Her elegant hands sweep upward like she's conducting an orchestra. "I think it was my Lutheran upbringing as well as a puritanical ethic ... work before pleasure. My parents weren't poor, but nothing was handed to you." She places her hands on her lap. "I always knew what I wanted to do and that did not include getting married to a pig farmer and having kids." Another smile. "I knew I wasn't meant to be a spectator but to participate, to be a runner in the marathon of life."

Her longest marathon—a powerful metaphor—a race open to everyone if they choose. A grinding, painful event of hills and wind, an unknown finish line, a zen-like acceptance of the journey.

The front door opens and Don walks in. Joyce smiles, a loving one, her partner and soul-mate. After a brief conversation, he heads to the kitchen to prepare dinner with the salmon he caught during a recent Alaskan fishing trip. Joyce continues.

"I'm so fortunate. My life is filled with wonderful people ... Don, Peter, my grandchildren, friends and wonderful co-workers."

And what about Peter, has he changed?

"Oh yes, he's happy, doesn't smoke or drink, and is off of all medications." A proud smile. "He's a supervisor at work now."

I hesitate for a moment before asking her, "Have he and his grandfather reconciled?"

Joyce ponders the question. "I wouldn't call it reconciliation, more like an understanding. When we went to Minnesota this summer, he and my father fished and played cards, just like old times. They didn't need to discuss things, just get back into life again."

"Like the bumps in a road—bounce off and continue going?"

"Yes," she says grinning. "Kind of like that."

It's time to go. Joyce and Don have their evening planned. Joyce stands.

"You know, yesterday was the six year anniversary."

I'm confused at first, and slightly embarrassed, like forgetting someone's birthday. Then it becomes clear. Yesterday was October 20th, six years after the accident, but Joyce announces it proudly and without anger or remorse, just another notch in her belt of life.

"We all have the ability to change. It's deep within us. We just have to find it."

Her mantra, her philosophy, her guiding light. A hug and out the door, although this is not the end. A mutual relationship based on trust, strong and everlasting, like Joyce herself. Reflecting back, it was the first meeting that still registers; total strangers at first, good friends after two hours—the image of Joyce walking to her car, away from the handicap parking, strong and directed, deliberately gracious with the slightest of limps, almost imperceptible.

Medical Records from Beacon Health

Beacon Health Limited, The Woodlands, Texas

Patient name: Joyce Lance

Physician: Ralph B. Lilly, MD

History of present illness: Joyce Lance is a 52-year-old female admitted on 11/13/2000 after being transferred from Hermann Hospital, after being involved in a high-impact motor vehicle-pedestrian crash. Her trauma resulted in poly-orthopedic and cranial injuries.

The patient had a right femur fracture, grade III, right tibia-fibula fracture, right knee wound, right shoulder dislocation, right distal radius fracture, a femoral fracture on the left, left fibular head fracture, T4 body burst fracture. She also has an abdominal compartment syndrome and had a laparotomy with a vacuum pump that is healing. She had multiple facial fractures, lacerations, C3 spinous process fracture, C2 burst fracture with halo placement, right zygomatic arch fracture, posterior frontal skull fracture, bilateral frontal contusions, pneumocephalus, and a right brachial plexopathy.

The postoperative neurological rehabilitation at Beacon has been complicated but the patient continues to do exceptionally well, participating with her pain management, management of her donor site, management of her halo, and the appropriate management for out of bed and physical activities that have been warranted. Eventually, the patient's tracheotomy was removed and she was eating fully. Over period of time, she was able to improve her healing status from the C2, so that the halo was removed.

The patient was seen for reevaluation orthopedically. The physicians involved, Dr. Tucker and Dr. Melissinos, followed with further surgical treatments with flaps required for her donor site which has not healed entirely. She was readmitted to Hermann Hospital, her fixators were taken off the tibia-fibula fractures. The patient was seen and treated by Dr. Melissinos and a graft was placed at the scalp wound and a graft was placed at the donor site.

PAST MEDICAL HISTORY: Essentially unremarkable. The patient has had a long career of taking care of her body, exercising, and actually has been a marathon runner. She has a high level executive function.

SOCIAL HISTORY: No history of alcohol or substance abuse.

PHYSICAL EXAMINATION:

GENERAL: The patient is alert, responsive, oriented. She is relatively cheerful and has insight into the complicating residuals from trauma.

VITAL SIGNS: Stable

HEENT: Intact

NECK: The soft Philadelphia collar is in place. The patient has been instructed regarding the outline of wound care management that Dr. Melissinos has made and limitation placed on her regarding her out of bed activities.

SKIN: Wound care: For the thigh, clean the medial aspect every day with hydrogen peroxide and half normal saline, apply Xeroform, cover with two Kerlix and place with ACE bandage. Change daily unless completely flat or dry. She has been cleansing the right lower extremity soft small wounds with half hydrogen peroxide and half normal saline, apply Xeroform and over with Kerlix and ACE bandage every day. Her scalp wound will be managed by cleaning wounds with hydrogen peroxide and normal saline, and Bacitracin.

HEART: Regular, no murmurs, no bruits.

CHEST: Clear

ABDOMEN: Soft, nontender with no masses.

MUSCULOSKELETAL: Deferred. The patient is limited in movement and has dressings and braces in place.

IMPRESSION:

1. Status post incision and drainage with graft placement and donor site in right thigh.
2. Status post incisions and drainage scalp wound with graft placement.
3. Status post motor vehicle-pedestrian accident with poly-orthopedic injuries.
4. Status post motor vehicle-pedestrian trauma with traumatic brain injury, severe.

PLAN:

1. Admission orders include those for wound care planning.
2. At present, her pain is being controlled with as-needed medications, including intravenous morphine sulfate if necessary, hyrdrocodone if necessary, and acetaminophen if necessary.
3. The patient's antibiotic program includes cephazolin 1 gram intravenous every eight hours, stop date is 3/05/01.
4. The patient will be seen by Dr. Valena, physical medicine and rehabilitation.

BEACON HEALTH LIMITED, THE WOODLANDS, TX

PATIENT NAME: Joyce Lance

PHYSICIAN: Nelson Valena, MD

REASON FOR CONSULTATION: Impaired gait

PHYSICAL EXAMINATION:

NEUROLOGICALLY: The patient is alert and following commands.

EXTREMITIES: She has limited range of motion in her right shoulder, abduction and forward flexion. She is able to extend her elbow to almost full extension. She has some difficulty with elbow flexion; however, she is able to touch her nose with her index finger. She has limited finger flexion bilaterally, right greater than left. She had limited knee flexion on the left. Her right lower extremity is difficult to examine secondary to the restrictions on her range.

SKIN: Her skin graft wounds are healing well. There is a small area of impaired skin granulation in the right skin donor site. However overall it looks clean and healthy. She had multiple skin grafts on her right lower extremity pin sites and her right scalp, which are clean.

MOTOR: Her strength is 4/5 in the right upper extremity except for the finger flexors. Left is 4+/5 throughout. Left lower extremity exam is limited secondary to her contractures. However, she is at least 2-3/5 throughout her left lower extremity. Right lower extremity is limited. However, she is able to dorsiflex and ankle plantar flex at least 2-3/5.

IMPRESSION: Multiple fractures status post auto-pedestrian accident with recent revision right donor skin graft and pin sites in her right lower extremity and her scalp. The patient also underwent recent removal of the right external fixator.

PLAN: We will resume activities with the following restriction:

1. Her right lower extremity is to be in a Bledsoe brace at all times except during dressing changes as recommended by orthopedics.
2. No active range of motion on her right lower extremity to prevent tension on the right lower extremity skin grafts.
3. Bed activities only until cleared by plastic surgery to increase movement in the right lower extremity.
4. Touchdown weight bearing only during transfers in bilateral lower extremities.
5. No CPM on the left. Only active and passive range of motion to prevent tension on the right lower extremity.
6. Rolling during bed mobility to prevent tension on the skin grafts.

GOALS OF THERAPY:

1. Concentrate on upper extremity strengthening.
2. Maintain range of motion in the left lower extremity and increase range of motion in the right upper extremity by using a Dyna splint on the right upper extremity.

3. Concentrate on endurance exercises such as ergometry exercise.
4. Avoid edge-of-bed activities for now to prevent any injury to the right skin grafts.
5. Continue isometric strengthening and ankle pumps bilaterally.

DISPOSITION: Patient is to follow up with Dr. Melissinos and Dr. Tucker for advancement in activities. I will follow up with you and increase therapies as she improves. Thank you for the consult.

PSYCHOLOGY 3/5/01

Patient's mood and affect seem generally improved. However, patient and nurse explained she is required to stay on bed rest for approximately one week and that she can only sit up in bed for about an hour at a time. Therefore, we'll need to arrange neuro-psychology testing around this. Will return on 3/7/01.

PSYCHIATRY 3/6/01

Reviewed patient's response and behavior for recent medical procedures and current bed rest limitations. Discussed patient's coping attitude and adjustment process. Patient emotionally managing well and maintaining health appropriate to current situation. Patient continues to benefit from supportive counseling.

PSYCHOLOGY 3/7/01

Neuropsych testing continues—patient tired after about an hour and requested that we continue another time. Hopeful, will complete testing later next week with report to follow. Will return 3/9.

PSYCH 3/9/01

Patient seen for follow up. Patient coping well and recent medical procedures and feedback on progress. Patient's mood improved with more realistic attitude and expectations. Continued with hypnotherapy procedure for healing, body image, and pain management. Patient responded well and encouraged to practice at frequent intervals.

NEURO 3/09/01

Reviewed with staff. She is bright, alert, participating. Today, up in wheelchair. Wound team working daily. She is building strength, endurance.

PSYCHOLOGY 3/12/01

Neuropsych testing continues. Will test memory and academic function next.

NEURO 3/12/01

Alert and cheerful. Scalp flap well healed. Other wounds significantly improved. Endurance improved.

PSYCH 3/13/01

Patient seen for follow up. Mood and affect significantly improved with significant decrease in depression and anxiety. Patient more clearly confident of herself now with greater acceptance of injuries and recovery process. Patient also more appropriately exerting control in available areas. Patient is adjusting very well and is currently emotionally stable. Patient reports making positive use of practice of self-hypnosis techniques for pain management and healing. Due to patient's progress, decision made by mutual agreement to reduce visit to once per week.

PHYSICAL MEDICINE AND REHAB 3/15/01

Doing well. Continues to be in good spirits. Improving in transfers with wheelchair mobility. Increase use of Right upper extremity. Wound/skin graft healing. Agree with trying to taper Effexor.

PSYCHOLOGY 3/16/01

Attempted to continue with neuropsych testing. Patient politely declined saying she was tired from AM visit to doctor's office.

PSYCHOLOGY 3/19/01

Attempted to continue testing. Patient politely declined for the second time in a row because her son was visiting and she "had to discuss something with him." Consequently, neuropsych testing is taking an inordinate length of time (patient also says she tires quickly, thus affecting her performance and slowing the process down). Will continue again this week.

PSYCH 3/20/01

Patient seen for follow up. Continuing to adjust well to recovery demands. Depression appears to be substantially reduced with patient exhibiting brighter affect and increased socialization. Patient applying coping strategies effectively in all areas.

PHYSICAL MEDICINE AND REHAB 4/3/01

No complaints. Doing well in therapy. Now able to ambulate several steps with platform. Slight improvement in finger contracture. Continue with physical and occupational therapy to increase ambulation. Continue with speech and psych for cognitive support.

PSYCHOLOGY 4/4/01

Patient continues with neuropsych testing—executive functioning assessed today. Testing will be completed on Friday 4/16

PSYCHOLOGY 4/16

Neuropsych testing completed. Report to follow

PSYCH 4/17

Patient reports significant increase in both therapeutic activities and life activities without significant difficulties noted. Patient denies observation of any cognitive difficulties in performance of work/tasks. Patient also denies any symptoms of post-traumatic stress disorder. Began discussion of adjustment issue to counselor as patient begins to anticipate discharge to home.

HOME EVALUATION 4/12/01

WHO WILL BE LIVING WITH PATIENT AT HOME? Son (Peter)

PATIENT MOBILITY: Wheelchair bound; ambulates with rolling walker

TYPE OF HOME: Single story

APPROACH TO HOME: Cement

IS SIDEWALK PRESENT LEADING TO THE ENTRANCE? Yes

LOCATION OF ENTRANCE TO BE USED BY PATIENT: Front. Will need assistance with wheelchair for small step

LIVING ROOM:

Can furniture be reorganized to allow for safer mobility? Yes

Comments: Rearrange fish tank—allow room for wheel-chair, and throw rugs will need to be removed to avoid tripping.

DINING ROOM: Will patient be using the table? Yes

KITCHEN: Will patient be involved with kitchen activities: No

BEDROOM:

Can patient reach night stand? Yes

Can patient reach telephone? Yes

Will patient be using a bedside commode? No

Is bathroom accessible from bedroom? Yes

Comment: Will rearrange fish tank to allow access to bed from right side.

BATHROOM:

Is the bathroom accessible with use of wheelchair? No

Assistive device? Yes

Height of toilet seat: 14.5 inches

Height of tub rim from floor: 21 inches

Comment: Recommend using guest bathroom for bath with use of tub bench, long handled shower nozzle, and grab bars. Will need raised toilet seat with at-tached grab bars.

LAUNDRY:

Will patient be involved with laundry responsibilities? No

IS TRANSPORTATION AVAILABLE? Yes. Son.

DISCHARGE SUMMARY: 4/27/01

Patient evaluated and received functional training, gait training, therapeutic exercise, standing balance activity, fam-ily training with wheelchair mobility training. Equipment ordered: 16 x16 wheelchair with elevating leg rests and re-movable arm rests; slinging board; rolling walker with 5 inch wheels

Outpatient physical therapy was recommended.

Patient was given list of outpatient therapy clinics close to her home. Family will be taking care of patient.

NURSING NOTES 4/27/01:

Patient is discharged to home with belongings. Escorted by friend via wheelchair. Patient is excited and in a good mood.

About
the Author

RANDY BIRKEN was born in 1950 and received a B.A. cum laude from Adelphi University in 1972 and a medical degree from Boston University in 1976. He completed his residency in Obstetrics and Gynecology at Baylor College of Medicine while serving as chief resident in 1980. Board certified in 1982 and re-certified in 1995, he is a fellow of the American College of Obstetricians and Gynecologists as well as the American College of Surgeons. In addition to his private practice in gynecology, uro-gynecology, and laparoscopic pelvic surgery, he is an Assistant Clinical Professor of Obstetrics and Gynecology at Baylor College of Medicine.

In 1997, Dr. Birken enrolled as a graduate student at Houston Baptist University and completed his Master in Liberal Arts degree in August of 2000. He has taught undergraduate literature as well as lecturing to medical students on literature with medical themes.

Medical publications have appeared in the *Journal of Obstetrics and Gynecology, Ob-Gyn News, Obstetrics and Gynecology,* and the *Journal of Reproductive Medicine.* Dr. Birken has published a short story in the "Internal Milieu" section of the *Archives of Internal Medicine,* a poem entitled "In a Candle's Flame" within a collection entitled *The Wounded Heart,* an essay in the *Journal of Graduate Liberal Studies* entitled "Painted Poetry: Charles Demuth's Visual Interpretation of William Carlos Williams "The Great Figure'," and a short story in the 2004 issue of *Dermanities* entitled "Court Room Medicine: Without a Pulse or Conscience." *A Harvard Death and Other Stories* (2006) is a collection of short stories published by Blue Dolphin, as well as *Women Only: Clinical Stories by a Gynecologist* (2009).

In addition to his love for literature, teaching, and writing, he is an avid cyclist, fitness enthusiast, golfer, baseball aficionado, pianist, and amateur radio operator. Dr. Birken has three sons, Tim, Mike, and Kyle. He and his wife, Liz, live in The Woodlands, Texas.

Made in the USA